Rudolf Steiner on Leonardo's *Last Supper*

The connection of Jesus, the cosmic Christ, and the 12 disciples, to the Zodiac

Adrian Anderson Ph. D.

Re-imaging the original Leonardo painting

Threshold Publishing, Australia 2017
www.rudolfsteinerstudies.com

Distributed by Dennis Jones P/L - Port Campbell Press
Bayswater VIC
Australia

ISBN 978-0-6481358-0-7 paperback
ISBN 978-0-6481358-1-4 hardback

Contents

꽃

Illustration Acknowledgments

Other books by the Author & website information

Illustrations   **page**

.....a magical quality emanates from this painting. The painting itself contributes, at most, only half of its magical quality; for it is **the Idea** which exerts an influence on the soul, and this has a mighty impact.

– Rudolf Steiner   (GA 62, lecture, 13th Feb. 1913)

The twelve Disciples correspond to the twelve zodiac signs; the zodiac forces which, together, are exerting an influence that is forming humanity. What is up there, above in the zodiac stars – this comes to expression in these twelve specific personalities.

– Rudolf Steiner   (Archive document, undated)

Foreword

Leonardo's great painting in Milan, as re-created through a series of restoration projects, is known throughout the world; it was one of most significant paintings to have come into the world, a wonderful gift to humanity. Indeed the Italian Renaissance with its superb paintings and architecture, particularly evident in Florence, forms a short episode in history which was like the brief blossoming of rare and exquisite flowers. Rudolf Steiner indicated generally that the souls who achieved this had been in a previous life either initiated in the Mysteries of the Hellenistic world, or blessed by exposure to the spiritual-cultural enrichment that the Mysteries had nurtured. As he told one audience, "the greatness of the Renaissance derives from spiritual impulses from ancient Greece {*from an incarnation in ancient Greece*}".[1] In regard to Leonardo specifically, he commented,

> To Spiritual-science, Leonardo da Vinci can really be termed a 'miracle man'; a person who is able to so perceive in such depths the immediate reality of the physical world as it reveals itself to our senses, that even in the disfigurement of his Last Supper painting, as it now exists in the church at Milan, it still speaks deeply to us, and also speaks to us out of the art prints which are available of it.[2]

Although the re-constituted version on display in Milan today, and the various versions available of it, as art-prints, still have a special quality, the theme of this book is not so much the actual painting by the great Leonardo, as such, but rather the spiritual Idea, or 'thought-form', which Leonardo experienced, and was then inspired to paint. The Idea of the painting is exactly that which Rudolf Steiner pointed out as the core value of the painting. He taught that it is partly the high quality of Leonardo's artwork, but more so the messages about deep and sacred meanings of esoteric Christianity which the Idea of the painting conveys, that make it so valuable,

> ...a magical quality emanates from this painting. The painting itself contributes, at most, only half of its magical quality; for it is **the Idea** which exerts this influence on the soul, and this has a mighty impact.[3]

The distinction between the original painting and the Idea of it is important, because the painting fell into ruin about 40 years after it was finished. But, Rudolf Steiner was aware that the tradition has saved 'the Idea' of Leonardo's painting for posterity. For in this tradition not only are there valuable reports from people in previous centuries about the painting but, much more importantly, a superb exact copy was made of the painting before it decayed. Rudolf Steiner commented about the damaged state of the original, and the tradition associated with it,

> ...of the painting of the Last Supper by Leonardo in the refectory of a monastery in Milan, today one sees actually only a series of moist dabs and specks of colour. Thus, to **really see what the painting portrayed, one has to obtain this from the tradition**. But today I don't intend to speak about {*what is available from*} the tradition, but other aspects...[4]
> (emphasis mine, AA)

When Rudolf Steiner wanted to show his audiences an illustration of the Last Supper painting, he made use of what the tradition has handed down to us. That is, he chose a magnificent engraving which faithfully reproduces the superb copy painted by an artist known as Giampetrino. In Rudolf Steiner's lifetime there were no art prints available of Giampetrino's copy, but it was from this painting that the engraving was made, copies of which were reproduced, and which Rudolf Steiner chose to illustrate his lectures. The engraving was by a brilliant Italian artist, called Raphaello Morghan (1758-1833) who moved to Florence in 1793,

---

[1] GA 171, 16th Sept. 1916.
[2] GA 61, lecture, 15th Feb. 1912, p. 360.
[3] GA 62, lecture, 13th Feb. 1913.
[4] Unlisted archive document; lecture, 28th Feb. 1913.

and a few years later, was commissioned by the Grand duke of Florence to make an engraving of the Last Supper painting **as copied by Giampetrino**. We know that Morghan copied the painting by Giampetrino, for only in this painting, and thus in the engraving, can important details from Leonardo's original work be seen; such as the salt container knocked over by Judas, and the almost transparent glass decanters.

There was only one other painting with all these details, but that was far away, in Belgium. The Giampetrino copy was in Italy; as late as 1626 it is recorded that this painting was in a church in the town of Pavia.[5] It is a sign of the intuitive capacity of Giampetrino that he also made a copy of another esoteric painting by Leonardo, the *Madonna of the Rocks*, of which there are two versions. The first version is the original esoteric painting, now in the Louvre. But there is another, inferior, version, now in London, which has lost its esoteric message through the alterations made to the scene.[6]

This use by Rudolf Steiner of Giampetrino's copy, via the Morghan engraving, is the same approach which I am taking in this book; except that in today's world, art prints and electronic images of paintings are readily available, so there is no need to detour via the Morghan engraving. The value of the Giampetrino copy cannot be exaggerated. Without it, much of the detail of the original would have been lost forever. In fact, as part of the tradition surrounding the Last Supper, two master artists had each been commissioned to paint an exact, full-size copy. When, on a computer, these two images are carefully refreshed and merged with the outer area of what was once Leonardo's painting in Milan, we can see very clearly how Leonardo's painting originally appeared – and this conveys to us the Idea, the astral image which Leonardo was perceiving, if not his own unique brush-strokes.

This re-creating process, of merging the copies into the original framework, which I have undertaken, has produced the image which will be used throughout this book. This is the best way to really experience this painting (the Idea behind it), and to experience what Leonardo's painting would have looked like originally. This Idea is of immense value to every soul who is seeking to sense the significance of Christianity, especially its cosmic aspects. In the light of Rudolf Steiner's words about Leonardo, and especially his unpublished spiritual research about the relationship of the Disciples to the zodiac, a relationship which is embedded in the painting, we can explore the profound esoteric meanings of this great painting.

The notes of this archive document, preserved in the Rudolf Steiner Archives in Dornach, form a crucial part of this book. The brief notes taken down of this lecture make no mention of the painting by Leonardo, but its theme is very closely allied to his Last Supper painting. These notes convey a deep cosmic view of Christianity, presenting insights about the zodiac and Christ and his disciples, which Leonardo could not have attained by himself. The deeply esoteric, cosmic Christianity presented in this painting is only really understood through anthroposophy, and in particular through the wisdom preserved in this archive document. Rudolf Steiner reveals the link between the zodiac and the Logos, and the zodiac and Jesus Christ, and also his twelve disciples. The full text of this priceless document is being made available in this book, and forms the basis of my commentary on the painting. It appears that nothing from this priceless document has ever before been published in anthroposophical circles; it is here translated in full.[7] (To preserve the legal copyright for the Rudolf Steiner Archives, regarding the German original, the German text is not being published here.)

As Rudolf Steiner commented about Leonardo and the Last Supper painting,

---

[5] This painting was earlier attributed to Marco d'Oggiono, but later to Giampetrino. Italian author B. Sanese mentions it was then in a monastery, the Certose, in Pavia. Decades after Morghan's work, the painter G. Bossi made a copy for Napoleon's mistress, Eugene de Beauharnais, but it is much inferior.
[6] The London version has, amongst other alterations, placed a staff in the hands of one of the two boys, thus making him into John the Baptist.
[7] For example, Michael Ladwein's fine book *Leonardo da Vinci, The Last Supper*, (Temple Lodge, UK, 2004).

The artist doesn't always know the secret content that has been hidden within his painting. The impelling downwards {*from high realms*}, of his astral visions did not have to penetrate through to his earthly awareness, to be able to live in what he paints. So perhaps Leonardo did not know of the hidden spiritual dynamics through which his painting came into being, that is not the main thing, but acting out of his instinctive feelings, he responded to these impulses {*from the spiritual source inspiring him*}.[8]

On another occasion Rudolf Steiner told an audience, "Images coming from the spiritual realms, were delivered over to great artists, such as Raphael, Michelangelo and Leonardo".[9] These inspiring impulses from spiritual realms are what convey the Idea of the painting to the artist. Leonardo da Vinci was, as Rudolf Steiner taught, a soul reincarnated from a lifetime in the glory days of ancient Greece, where the Mysteries flourished.[10] Indeed, in a lecture dedicated to this artist, Rudolf Steiner revealed that Leonardo had been an initiate in the Hellenistic Age. He explains that in the Renaissance, Leonardo was unable to manifest his full spiritual capacity because of difficulties connected to the impediments which a modern body (and culture) presents to high spiritual consciousness.[11] But it is still possible for such souls to be blessed with inspirational insights from spiritual realms.

In addition to such gifted souls as Leonardo having a capacity to intuit artistic images with deep meaning, there is another special factor that can help them to bring about great artistic works. Rudolf Steiner indicates that a great saint, or high initiate, known as Christian Rosencreutz, who in medieval times brought about a deeper, esoteric understanding of Christianity, known as the Rosicrucian movement, also subtly inspires such gifted souls in their work. This great spiritual leader of the medieval Rosicrucians helps to guide the cultural-spiritual development of the western world. It is my conclusion that the Last Supper painting by Leonardo can be regarded as an example of this activity; enabling him in this way to create a painting which embodies profound truths of a cosmic, esoteric Christianity, that is, a Rosicrucian Christianity. Throughout this book, I shall be endeavouring to unveil the high Christian initiatory truths within this painting.

The painting that is now known around the world as the *Last Supper* is not the painting which was originally painted in Milan by Leonardo, just before 1500 AD. This was lost to the world by 1550, because it was destroyed by dampness which, after a few short decades, crept up the wall of the building and caused the painting to decay, and then fall off the wall, in large chunks. The version of the Last Supper used here is also available as an art print, see my website,

www.rudolfsteinerstudies.com.

---

[8] GA 283 p. 26.
[9] GA 332a, lecture, Oct. 1919 p. 128.
[10] GA 171, lecture, 16th Sept. 1916.
[11] GA 62, lecture, 13th Feb. 1913.

1 The Last Supper as it probably looked in AD1500: merging the Giampetrino and Solario copies.

2 The R. Morghan engraving: from Giampetrino, early 1800's

Introduction: The background to the image used in this book

Leonardo was born in 1452 in the little town of Vinci in north Italy and he died on the 2nd of May, 1519. He was originally a student of Verocchio. His great painting was commissioned by the Duke Lodovico il Moro; it was painted on a wall of the Dominican convent of Saint Marie Delle Grazie in Milan, between the years 1495-98. When setting out to paint this great work, Leonardo decided to use a new and potentially superior method of painting onto a wall, known as 'secco', which allows one to paint on to dry plaster, so the artist need not hurry. But unlike the usual 'fresco' technique, his new technique was especially prone to serious decay, if it were exposed to moisture. Sadly, not only did the wall absorb dampness and thereby damage the painting, the entire building was once flooded. In addition, French soldiers were once quartered there, and these men threw rocks at the painting; and the monks living in the place once heightened the door in the rear wall, cutting into the remnants of the painting. Also, an heraldic shield was once put on the wall, up above the head of Christ.

By 1550 a great Renaissance artist, Vasari, reported, "Only blotches were left", and by 1595 these were all but gone. The painting which tourists see today in Milan is the result of at least eight restoration attempts, starting back in 1726, during which the painting was re-painted. Some projects took several years to complete, the more recent costing millions of dollars. In an earlier restoration and repainting, one restorer actually cut large pieces out of what was left of the original, not knowing that it was painted in the secco technique, thinking that therefore there would be a deeper layer of painting beneath it; but the wall underneath was of course, blank.

The alterations and restoration work in brief:

1 1726: First restoration attempt; Michelangelo Bellotti painted over the remnants then varnished it.

2 1770: Guiseppe Mazza reversed all of Bellotti's work and re-painted it again, but public outrage stopped the project.

3 1787: Abbate C. Bianconi, secretary of the Brera Academy reported that the painting "had suffered much having been barbarously renovated from top to bottom, so that all it retains of the Master's hand, is its composition {*the over-all scheme*}.[12]

4 1821: Stefano Barezzi cut off whole segments, as he did not know it was not the usual fresco, and as a result, all that he cut off – whole segments – were lost forever. He actually then went down onto the floor to pick up bits of the fallen flakes of paint, and then glued these back onto the wall.

5 1901- 08: Luigi Cavenagh cleaned the fragments left.

> Rudolf Steiner commented in 1913 about the effects of the restoration efforts up to this point, "Through artistic charlatanry, it has been re-painted: this is how one has to describe it...today there is just a shadow left, but a magical quality still emanates from it..." [13]

6 1924: Oreste Silvestri cleaned and stabilized the bits remaining.

7 1951-54: Mauro Pellicciolli did the same as Silvestri before him.

---

[12] M. Ladwein, *Leonardo da Vinci, the Last Supper*...p.96.
[13] GA 62, lecture, 13th Feb. 1913, p.356.

8 1978-99: Giampetrino Pinin Barcilon used sophisticated instruments to find the original outlines, and to find flakes of the original and to then **repaint the figures himself**.

So, restorers over some 250 years literally re-drew the picture themselves, as best they could, assisted by reference to the tradition (that is, earlier copies). Unfortunately, all this work could only result in a patchy and incomplete final picture. But this patchy result is often artificially completed, to produce finished, polished versions, which are needed for commercial and religious markets.

The most recent efforts at restoration have improved on that, but it remains still a re-painting activity which seeks futilely, in honour of Leonardo, to replace the superb Giampetrino copy.

Giampetrino
That we can know exactly how this painting looked is due to the magnificent copy made in 1520 by Giampetrino, an abbreviation for Giovanni Pietro Rizzoli, (1495-1549). Giampetrino was a pupil of Leonardo, and he painted his copy with oil paints on canvas. It is my conclusion that this copy is virtually identical to what was painted by Leonardo. The reasons are firstly, a patron would naturally want an exact copy, one that would perfectly resemble the original; and it is considered highly likely that Giampetrino actually worked with Leonardo on painting the Last Supper in Milan, as he was a student of the great master. Secondly, this intention for a perfect copy is confirmed by the choice of Giampetrino, because he was famed for his ability to make truly perfect duplicates of any Renaissance painter's work.

Another great artist also made a copy between 1508-1508, which is now in a monastery in Tangerlo, Antwerp, in Belgium. This copy, which is attributed to Andrea Solario, has exactly the same features as that of the one painted by Giampetrino. These two paintings, being so similar, establish that they each depict accurately what Leonardo had painted. This conclusion is also that of the famed Professor of Art History, E. H. Gombrich, through whose enthusiasm and influence, the Giampetrino copy, which had been acquired by the London Royal Academy Art Gallery in 1821, was placed on display in Oxford University (high up in a corridor area in Magdalen College).

However, the Giampetrino painting has had its outer areas cut off at some time in its history; that is, the ceiling of the room and some of the outer parts of the walls were removed. Also, over centuries of being exposed to candle soot, this copy became somewhat darker..

Over long hours of work, I have tried to lighten the darkened areas and reduce the bluish tone, and to then merge this image into the outer area of the original painting in Milan by Leonardo. This outer area had been re-created very well by art restorers, again by them using the Giampetrino and Solario copies. My extensive work to clarify and improve the image was further helped by the decision of the London Gallery which owns the Giampetrino copy, The Royal Academy of the Arts, to improve their copy by merging the well preserved lower section from the Solario copy in Belgium, especially the area depicting the feet of the people at the table. The result is, I believe, an accurate re-creation of how the original painting would have appeared; and hence a reliable version of the spiritual 'imaginative' image or Idea of the painting.

We shall now contemplate the deeper meanings of the spiritual Idea which we know as "the Last Supper", using the image I have formed from the Royal Academy version and the other sources mentioned.

Chapter One: Esoteric Christianity and the Last Supper

The painting by Leonardo is about a crucial moment in a sacred, ritualistic meal which Jesus celebrated with his Disciples, shortly before he was arrested and killed. To discover what initiatory wisdom sees in this painting, we need to briefly consider the main elements of esoteric Christianity and gain a clear understanding of the context of this Last Supper. The true sequence of events, from the Last Supper up to the arrest and trial of Jesus, which ended in the Crucifixion, has long been a controversial subject. This is because the accounts of this sequence of events in the synoptic Gospel writers, and in that by St. John, seem to be inconsistent. It was argued, for example, that the Synoptic Gospels indicate the Last Supper occurred on the Passover Day, (a Friday), and not, as in the Gospel of John, on the Thursday.

The Sequence of Events

My view is that there is no real discrepancy in the four reports, because the Synoptic writers when reporting the discussion between them and Jesus about celebrating the Passover, were of the understanding that this would be their especial Passover, and not the official one. They must have had this understanding because they were asked to prepare for this sacramental meal, so that they could celebrate it together, on a day prior to the actual, official age-old Passover day. They obviously could not celebrate the official Passover with other persons as the Jewish authorities were seeking to arrest Jesus. But they need not have celebrated the Passover on the 'wrong' day.

It was obvious to them, if somewhat puzzling, that their Passover meal would be especially arranged and timed as required by the directives of Jesus, to be held on the wrong day. The purpose behind this unusual Passover meal was to bring about a hugely significant symbolic statement. This understanding that it was a special Passover festival, for a new specific purpose, which would centre on the nature of Jesus, is indicated in the Gospel of St. Matthew,

> Mt 26:17 On the first day of the Feast of Unleavened Bread, the disciples **came to** Jesus saying, "Where do you want us to make preparations **for you** to eat the Passover?"

This report shows a very specific approach being undertaken by Jesus, and then emphasizes that this Passover would be done as Jesus wished. Because the text could have, and normally would have, just said,

> On the first day of the Feast of Unleavened Bread, the disciples asked Jesus, "Where do you want us to make preparations to eat the Passover?"

It was the intention of Jesus to enact a ritualistic meal on the day **before** the Jews gathered to have their Passover Festival. This event would be a kind of Passover meal, but a **new** kind of Passover meal. St. Luke reports that Jesus himself referred to it as a Passover meal, but obviously he was not using this term in the traditional, 'legal' sense, since it was not going to be the usual ritual meal. It would be a Passover meal, but of a different kind being celebrated on a different day; the words of Jesus as they begin their special Passover event, in St. Luke's account quite clearly show this, "*I have earnestly desired to eat the Passover meal with you, before I suffer.*" (Lk, 22:15) This Last Supper, also known as the Lord's Supper, took place on Thursday, the day **before** the Jewish people celebrated their Passover supper.

It was in the evening of Thursday, the 2nd April in AD 33, a day now known as Maundy Thursday, that Jesus and his Disciples gathered together to carry out a truly remarkable ritual meal. In the evening of the next day, Friday, the Jewish Passover Festival was to be celebrated, this was the time when Jews in Palestine would have a solemn ritualistic evening meal, to commemorate the day when their forefathers were released from Egypt, by Moses about 1,300 years before. For this ritual meal, a lamb was slaughtered, then cooked and consumed in a meal together with bitter herbs, a fruit puree sauce, and unleavened bread. The Jewish people understood that when consuming the flesh of the sacrificial lamb in this ritualistic way, they were to remember the great event in their history, of Jahve-God ensuring that their ancestors were released from Egypt. But also, that carrying out this ritual would reconcile them to God, and He would ensure they would continue to be looked after, just as their ancestors in Egypt were protected from the sequence of plagues that devastated Egypt, by having the blood of a lamb above the door of their houses. But earlier on this particular Friday, now known as Paschal Day or Easter Friday, Jesus will be arrested, interrogated, put on trial, scourged, and then crucified. It was on the Thursday evening before all this, that the 'Last Supper' took place.

What kind of event was this ? The Gospel account tells us that the disciples were directed to gather at a special room for this event. Rudolf Steiner revealed that "this was a room used for initiation purposes",[14] and in fact, he is referring to the Essenes, some of whom lived in Jerusalem.[15] (Only a small number of Essenes lived at their centre in Qumran.) So, firstly, we note that the Last Supper occurred in a very special, sacred place. Secondly, we need to note that this ritual meal had some, but only some, elements to it which were similar to those of the Passover meal. For example, both events commenced with initial words of address from the leader of the community: on this Thursday, these were from Jesus, and in the normal Passover, these were spoken by the highest ranking priest present. Also, on the Thursday occasion, and also in the Passover meal, there was a dipping of food into a fruit sauce, and the singing of hymns.

From the viewpoint of the Jewish priests, the meal on the Thursday would not have been a Passover meal by definition, because it did not take place on the Passover day (the next day, Friday, the 3rd of April). But, if they were told that the small group around Jesus viewed it as a kind of Passover event, the religious authorities would have regarded that as irreligious, and indeed as blasphemy. Because, firstly, it was the wrong day, and secondly because of the most striking difference between the Thursday 'Last Supper', and the traditional Passover meal. The primary symbolic item present at the normal Passover meal was the sacrificial lamb, which had been slaughtered the day before and then carefully cooked, but with the non-standard ritual meal that Jesus and the Disciples were to experience, as the painting by Leonardo depicts, there was no 'Passover lamb' on the table.

A Passover Lamb

This question as to whether there was, or was not, a slaughtered lamb on the table is disputed. Those who argue that there was a lamb, point to a passage in the Gospel of St. Mark, 14:12, to support their argument. But in fact the Greek here is ambiguous, and therefore translated differently according to what the translator has decided is the fact of the matter. Those who wish to believe that there was slaughtered lamb present, translate it dubiously as,

> On the first day of the Feast of Unleavened Bread, **when they {the Disciples} had sacrificed the Passover lamb,** Jesus' disciples asked him, "Where do you want us to go and make preparations for you to eat the Passover?"

But the Greek does **not** specify the Disciples; it uses an indefinite plural form of the verb ('people') and is in the simple past tense ('sacrificed'), not the perfect past tense ('had sacrificed'). So it actually means: **"when people sacrificed"** the Passover Lamb: (in the Greek, ὅτε τὸ πάσχα ἔθυον = *hoti to pascha ethuon.*)[16] This is in effect saying, "on the day when it was, and had been for centuries, the custom for people in Israel to sacrifice the Passover Lamb".

So it is accurately translated, in the NIV as,

---

[14] GA 97, p. 53 (Question & Answer session).
[15] Not, as Emil Bock writes in *The Three Years*, in "a Coenacolum" nor Upper (dining) room, nor in a small synagogue.
[16] In all the many ancient papyrus and other manuscripts of the Gospel, there are no alternative versions of this phrase; although there are many versions for some words in the four or five verses preceding verse 12.

^{Mk 14:12} On the first day of the Feast of Unleavened Bread, **when it was customary to sacrifice the Passover lamb,** Jesus' disciples asked him, "Where do you want us to go and make preparations for you to eat the Passover?"

There was no lamb on the table, because Jesus Christ was indicating to them, that he was to become the new sacrificial lamb: the "Lamb of God", as announced by John the Baptist some three years earlier at the Baptism in the Jordan. The Disciples did not need the additional time to slaughter and cook a lamb; so they could make arrangements for the meal on that same day. Instead, Jesus spoke the immensely mysterious and sacred words about the Disciples needing to drink from the cup, as if it were his blood, and eating of some bread, as if it were his body. What was happening ?

Jesus was signifying that he was a kind of higher Moses; someone who would lead all people who respond to his call, out of imprisonment in the material world (not just out of Egypt), however one may wish to understand this. Esoterically, it implies that those who seek spiritual development can conquer their lower self and rise above the various allures that the material or earth-bound reality offers. In this evening, Jesus inaugurated the ritual of consuming the wine and bread as if this was part of his being. He also spoke of the one who was to betray him, and in the longer report in St. Luke's Gospel, he spoke about the future tasks of the Disciples.

After the Last Supper, Jesus and the Disciples went out in the Garden of Gethsemane to pray; by now it was in the early hours of Friday morning. Soon, in the pre-dawn darkness, Judas Iscariot and the soldiers arrive. Jesus is arrested, as was pre-planned, and then subjected to a trial, then sent to Pilate, who reluctantly allowed the crucifixion of Jesus to be carried out. In the evening of this Friday, when the Jews were preparing their sacrificial lamb for the Passover meal, Jesus died; and as they were celebrating the Passover meal, the body of Jesus was laid in the grave, by Joseph of Arimathea.

Let's review the events of the end of the Holy Week:

THURSDAY 2nd April   AD 33   13th Nisan (in the Jewish calendar)
PM: the Last Supper occurs, as a new kind of Passover meal
There was a sharing of bread and wine
After the meal, the profoundly symbolic Foot-washing was carried out[17]
It is also the preparation day for the official Passover meal
The traitor Judas is pointed out by Jesus, and he goes out into the night
Jesus goes out to the Mt. Olives late in the night, to pray in the garden
of Gethsemane

(This going out into the night has far more significance than most readers would know, since it was understood in Judaism, that anyone who leaves their house on Passover night will be attacked by evil spirits. In this evening, Judas had become a servant of evil spirits, and Jesus will soon become the victim of evil forces.)

****

FRIDAY 3rd April   Easter/Paschal Day   14th Nisan   Passover Day
Pre-dawn: betrayed by the kiss of Judas, Jesus is arrested
Early Morning: He is put on trial, questioned by Pilate, scourged, and taken to Golgotha hill to be killed

---

[17] A unique archive document explaining the esoteric significance of the foot-washing is due for publication in 2018.

Noon: He is crucified
From noon to 3 pm: a mysterious darkness falls, and earthquakes occur

3 pm: The Death Of Jesus, which is preceded by the cry,
  "My deity, my deity, how thou hast glorified me"
  there is also the offering of vinegar

6 pm: Longinus pierces his body, releasing the spiritual energies of the cosmic sun-god
  into the earth
  The body is taken down from the cross
  Jesus is buried in the tomb
  Earthquakes continue intermittently

Sunset: The traditional **Passover** festival occurs now

****

SATURDAY 4ᵗʰ **April**   15ᵗʰ Nisan

He is in the tomb, and the Descent into Hades is undertaken

****

SUNDAY 5ᵗʰ **April**   16ᵗʰ Nisan

The Resurrection occurs

In the pre-dawn darkness, Mary Magdalene arrives at the tomb, and sees him. He was in his 'resurrection' body, so she does not recognize him until he speaks to her. The reason for this is, as Rudolf Steiner explains, that Jesus had enveloped the 'essence' of his physical body, in an especially dense etheric body, so that Mary, with a little etheric clairvoyance, could see him. (This 'resurrection body' is physical, but in the most delicate sense; it is devoid of protoplasm {flesh}, and hence has a somewhat ethereal, energy quality.[18])

In a very striking act of affirming the equality of women, and dismissing their inferior position in society, a woman had just been chosen by the resurrected Saviour, to testify about the stupendous event, from which Christianity itself would arise. (In Judaism at that time, the testimony of a woman, about anything, had no validity in any court.)

****

In summary: Friday April 3rd – Sunday April 5th, AD 33
Jesus was on the cross for about 4 to 6 hours
He was in the tomb for ¼ of Friday, all of Saturday, and ¼ of Sunday; this is chronologically, three days.

****

---

[18] That is, there is a difference between the 'flesh/material body' and the 'physical body' which has now been permeated by flesh, but it is in itself a form consisting of physical energies underpinned by an ethereal structure, called the 'phantom'.

11

An overview of esoteric Christianity

In this book we won't be considering in detail the immense significance of the Resurrection; the reader may already be aware of this from Rudolf Steiner. My introductory book to his teachings, *The Rudolf Steiner Handbook*, provides a chapter on this subject, incorporating references to the Greek text of the Gospels. But we do need to briefly mention here the essential points of esoteric Christianity, revealed though anthroposophy, and therefore of the Resurrection of Christ. As we explore the painting, the importance of the Christ-reality, as understood in esoteric Christianity, will be contemplated often. In anthroposophy, there is a cosmic view of Christianity; a great cosmic spiritual being 'the Christ' is seen as a separate being to the man, Jesus. This perspective is derived from the context of a very living and complex cosmos, wherein – above the physical-mineral world – nine ranks of divine beings exist. At the Resurrection, the cosmic 'Christ', permeated the planet's aura with a divine spiritual energy; this ensures the on-going existence of the Earth as an etheric body in the far future, long after its physical existence has died away.

As part of the cosmic Christianity that Rudolf Steiner taught, we have a striking description of the significance of the events on Golgotha, seen from a global perspective. He describes how one could view the Earth from a position far out in space, and go back in time, gazing down upon the planet over millennia. He described how one would thereby see the physical Earth enveloped in its oval shaped aura, which is filled with manifold colours and forms. Then at a particular moment, one would see that this aura suddenly changed. He explains that one then realizes that the Earth's aura has dramatically changed, and one discovers that "this is the moment when the blood flowed from the Redeemer" on Golgotha.[19]

This descent of the cosmic Christ also has enabled human beings who seek spirituality, to attain to spirituality; their purified and renewed astral body or aura, shall draw the higher, purer soul energies from the divine light now permeating the planet. And, the higher part of the human being, the human spirit, or 'Spiritual-self' is also enabled to develop. It shall transform its own small rudimentary divine potential, or 'devachanic' aura, into a large and glorious 'spirit-body' aura.

In addition, the human being who achieves spirituality, can now also start to imbue their life-forces or 'etheric body' with divine life-forces. This 'body' which currently maintains the health of the physical body, and underlies reproduction and sense perception, can transform into the 'Life-spirit'. The Life-spirit bestows profound artistic capacities and miraculous healing abilities on the person. It also results in a consciousness which gradually becomes eternal, that is, able to function in Devachan, the true, transcendent Heaven. These brief remarks give a glimpse into the significance of the events on Golgotha hill; events which were preceded by the Last Supper. The following extract from a lecture by Rudolf Steiner describes this very clearly,

> With the event on Golgotha, as the blood flowed from the wounds of the great Redeemer, as the Cosmic Heart's blood permeated the Earth, right into the core of the planet, the Earth started to glow; from deep within, light began to stream out, into the surrounds. Through this, the possibility was also given for each human individual to experience itself in this light. As the Earth became the body of the great sun-spirit, in that He permeated the planet with his spiritual forces, then all life on the planet was also given these forces. The physical body of Jesus of Nazareth was the mediator through which the forces for the cosmos streamed out at Golgotha...the human being can experience this light in itself as an earthly human being, as he or she recognizes himself or herself as a part of the Earth which is now the body of the cosmic Christ. [20]

And of course, on a more everyday level, the teachings and actions of Jesus, shall provide the highest ethical encouragement, to those who read the Gospels.

---

[19] GA 104, lecture, 24th June 1908.
[20] GA 265, p. 417.

The Lord's Supper
The account in the Gospel of St. Matthew of the Lord's Supper, describes an episode which led to the institution of what has become the holiest of sacraments for Christians, over some 2,000 years: the Eucharist or Holy Mass. From the Gospel of Matthew 26: 26-28,

> While they were eating, Jesus took bread, gave thanks and broke it, and gave it to his disciples, saying, "Take and eat; this is my body." [Mt 26:27] Then he took the cup, gave thanks and offered it to them, saying, "Drink from it, all of you. [Mt 26:28] This is my blood of the covenant, which is poured out, for many, for the forgiveness of sins.

It is precisely one of the mysteries in the Gospel of John that in his report of what happened in the Last Supper, this part of the evening is not included. As I mentioned in *The Hellenistic Mysteries and Christianity*, these words from St. Mathew's account are understood to mean that the individual worshipper may share spiritually in the very being of Jesus. Hence the sacredness of these words. So it is very striking to discover that these words and the associated action of passing around bread and wine, are entirely omitted in the Gospel of John. This omission has caused serious difficulties for theologians for many centuries. It seems to be a very serious defect in this Gospel.

The Lord's Supper in the Gospel of John
But once the deeper spiritual message in this Gospel is discerned, then this omission becomes understandable. Instead of affirming the spiritual union of **individual Christians with Jesus** (and his associated, but undefined, divine-ness), the writer of the Gospel of John has affirmed, in a veiled way, the esoteric truth of the spiritual union of the **cosmic Christ** with the **Earth-soul, and through this process, with humanity.**

For this reason, in this Gospel the sacramental words from the Last Supper about taking and eating the bread, or drinking wine, are omitted, because those words are directed to individuals in an ecclesiastical setting, wherein the congregation becomes the 'body', that is a part of the spiritual essence of Jesus Christ. But the description in the Gospel of John is about the larger, cosmic perspective wherein all individuals, even if unaware of this, are to become people who, in living on the planet, and so of course walking over it, shall become part of the body of the great cosmic Christ spirit who is about to become the indwelling spiritual essence of planet Earth.[21]

This deeper nature of the Gospel of John is shown in regard to the Last Supper, for its description of this event fills five chapters, in which further teachings of Christ are given; teachings that involve some of the deepest and most significant truths about the meaning of the Christ-impulse.

Consequently, the Gospel of John has a deeper, more esoteric perspective than the other Gospels. As Rudolf Steiner expressed this,

> But the deeper initiate, who could see much deeper into the true spiritual situation prevailing behind the sensory world, much deeper than the other three Evangelists, is the writer of the Gospel of John.[22]

It is the cosmic and esoteric aspects to the Christ-reality, with its associated zodiacal significance, and the role of evil in creation, which are the focus of the painting. To depict deeper aspects of the Christ-reality, St. John includes an incident involving Judas, which the other Gospels leave out. This is the account of the Last Supper in John's Gospel,

---

[21] There are references to this cosmic dimension in this Gospel, through the recording of the washing of the feet incident, which has to do with initiation and with Piscean energies; this matter will be explained in another book.
[22] GA 57, lecture of 14th Nov. 1980, *Bible and Wisdom* II.

The Gospel of John, 13: 18-28

Jn 13:18 "I am not referring to all of you; I know those I have chosen. But this is to fulfill the scripture: 'He who shares my bread has lifted up his heel against me."

Jn 13:19 "I am telling you now before it happens, so that when it does happen you will believe that I am He.

Jn 13:20 I tell you the truth, whoever accepts anyone I send accepts me; and whoever accepts me accepts the one who sent me."

Jn 13:21 After he had said this, Jesus was troubled in spirit and testified, "I tell you the truth, one of you is going to betray me."

Jn 13:22 His disciples stared at one another, at a loss to know which of them he meant.

Jn 13:23 One of them, the disciple whom Jesus loved, was reclining next to him.

Jn 13:24 Simon Peter motioned to this disciple and said, "Ask him which one he means."

Jn 13:25 Leaning back against Jesus, he asked him, "Lord, who is it?"

Jn 13:26 Jesus answered, "It is the one to whom I will give this piece of bread when I have dipped it in the dish." Then, dipping the piece of bread, he gave it to Judas Iscariot, son of Simon.

Jn 13:27 As soon as Judas took the bread, Satan entered into him. "What you are about to do, do quickly," Jesus told him, but no one at the meal understood why Jesus said this to him.

We shall be considering this account throughout the book, but especially the core words here, which the painting depicts,

> After he had said this, Jesus was troubled in spirit and testified, "I tell you the truth, one of you is going to betray me." His disciples stared at one another, at a loss to know which of them he meant. One of them, the disciple whom Jesus loved, was reclining next to him. Simon Peter motioned to this disciple and said, "Ask him which one he means."

The painting by Leonardo depicts precisely this dramatic incident, which only occurs in John's Gospel. But the composition or structure of the painting is such that it portrays this event in a way that indicates deep truths of esoteric Christianity to the viewer. In this incident, the Disciple known as Lazaros is involved. Before we begin to contemplate the secrets of this painting, we need to be clear about the especial nature of the Gospel of John, and the relation of Lazaros to this text. We also need to understand the involvement of Lazaros in the Lord's Supper on that Thursday evening, long ago.

14

Chapter Two: Lazaros and John's Gospel

The Gospel of John and who wrote it

It is significant that the painting of the Last Supper refers directly to an episode reported only in the Gospel of John, for it is this Gospel which provides a deeper perspective on the Christ-Mystery than that of the other three gospels, known as the 'Synoptic' gospels. This deeper perspective is shown right at the beginning where the Nativity of Jesus has been omitted, and instead, reference is made to a cosmic theme or a cosmic being: 'the Logos',

In the beginning was the Logos, and the Logos was inwardly with God, and a god was the Logos.
(transl. the author)

This term 'Logos' is normally translated as "the Word", and is understood to be an alternative name for Christ. Rudolf Steiner reveals that it refers to a sublime deity, we shall explore what this term means in more detail, later.

The person who wrote this Gospel was traditionally identified as 'St. John', meaning a Disciple of Christ, namely John the Apostle, the son of Zebedee. But Rudolf Steiner reports that Lazaros was the writer of what we call the Gospel of John. We may at first find this startling, but in fact this is simply because we have been influenced by an assumption going back some 1800 years, that it was the Apostle John who wrote this Gospel. This has no basis to it whatsoever, and in fact some theologians have reached the same conclusion as Rudolf Steiner. The reasons for discarding the Apostle John as the author are many and very solid. Theologians have long argued that there are quite a number of theological reasons to doubt that John the Apostle was the author. For example, there are three really significant moments in the life of Jesus, which the other Gospels tell us were witnessed by the Apostle John and two other Disciples (Peter and James). These are, the raising of the daughter of Jairus, the praying in the innermost part of the garden of Gethsemane and the Transfiguration. None of these three are even mentioned in the Gospel of John, let alone depict the Apostle John in a prominent role in these events. Not only that, but every single event in the three other Gospels where John is mentioned, is omitted from the Gospel of John. There are many other points that could be pointed out.

Lazaros -John

The most substantial basis for arguing that Lazaros-John was the author, was pointed out by Rudolf Steiner. His insightful reading of the Gospel, quite apart from what his seership revealed, shows us that the perspective on the Christ-reality embodied in this Gospel derives from an initiatory consciousness, only obtainable from an interaction with Jesus Christ, at a very deep level. In his lectures on this Gospel, Rudolf Steiner explains in detail how Lazaros-John provides indeed an eye-witness testimony, but from the eye of a seer also, not only as an historical witness. This gave him understanding of the events in the life of Jesus on a deep spiritual level.

But a major reason for the confusion about the authorship, known only to Rudolf Steiner, is that after Lazaros was initiated, his name was altered; **he became known as 'Lazaros-John'**. So it is this individual who wrote the Gospel of John, and the Book of Revelation; not that St. John, known as 'John the Apostle', who was the son of Zebedee, and brother of James the Great, and who is numbered amongst the 12 Disciples. Lazaros-John wrote his account from not only what his historical, personal involvement enabled him to do, but what the empowered higher consciousness (clairvoyance in the deepest sense) bestowed upon him by the Holy Spirit enabled him to achieve.

The reason for his name change is that the name 'John', although a common personal name, was also used as an esoteric name for those who were initiated. This is because the three vowels in this name in Greek, that is IAO, were experienced in this combination, as signifying divine beings, and when used in a name, it signified the presence of a high spiritual reality in a person.

At some point in the Hellenistic Age, they had become the core vowels for a name of a high deity, amongst people associated with the 'Mysteries', but also for Greek-speaking Jews. For these people, these three letters designated the name of God; replacing the JHVH name.[23] Sacred medallions and gemstones still exist with these three vowels engraved on them. There is a hint of this esoteric perspective in the Greek text of the Gospel of John, when John the Baptist is introduced in the beginning of the Gospel, and 'John' is emphasized,

> There was begotten a man, sent forth by God: {the} name of him, {was} 'John'.[24]

The sentence here could have been, "...*John the Baptist*" but it is simply left, somewhat abruptly, as simply "John", as if to emphasize this name. That his name is meant to signify this sacred, special meaning is indicated by a strangely out of place sentence in the Greek commentary on the Gospel of John, by the great Origenes, writing in the third century AD. He refers to Old Testament prophets when suddenly he writes, "The name "IAO" when interpreted means, 'being elated' or 'raised up'."[25] This sentence probably belongs back earlier in his text, when he refers to John the Baptist. It is indicating what Rudolf Steiner taught about this name John, with its three vowels.[26] He explained that these vowels for initiation purposes were being considered like this:

> **i** = striving towards god / deity
> **a** = the sublime nature of deity
> **o** = comprehending, nearing, God [27]

These interpretations are in fact what the planets induce in the astral body, at their highest level of influence. He also commented that the IAO is connected to how Christ is efficacious in human beings.[28] Rudolf Steiner reports that Lazaros had his named extended, or changed, to become known as "Lazaros-John", and this implies that it occurred in accordance with will of Christ Jesus. In this connection it is very significant to know that the Risen Jesus, in addressing Simon Peter also re-named him, (extended his name). Jesus usually refers to St. Peter as "Simon". This name change affecting Peter or Simon is recorded in the last chapter of the Gospel of John: the name "John" was added, making him in effect, 'Simon-John'. This occurred after he was successful at, or at least very strongly engaged in, the famous 'fishing' event which resulted in a catch of 153 fishes. (This story very discreetly refers to an initiatory challenge, which we cannot go into here.) At that point, a dialogue starts between Simon-Peter and the Risen Jesus,

> [Jn 21:15] When they had finished eating, Jesus said to Simon Peter, "Simon, son of John, do you truly love me more than these?"

It is unlikely that Peter's father was called John; at least, this is not mentioned anywhere, and in fact elsewhere Jesus refers to Simon Peter as the 'son of Jonah' (Matth. 16:17). But here, Jesus mysteriously changes 'Jonah' to 'John'. There is a subtle, but definite, difference between these two names. This re-naming is telling the perceptive reader that St. Peter (or Simon) has by now developed some higher spiritual qualities; we can say that 'Simon-John' has attained to some of the high spirituality which the name John points to.

In his first lectures on Christianity as 'a mystical fact', given in 1902, Rudolf Steiner reveals some facts from the Akashic Record, about the life of the great Lazaros-John and its unique importance. He reports that Lazaros-John, when living at Ephesus from mid- to late first century

---

[23] This use of IAO in this way, is written a small papyrus leaf from the 1st century AD, found amongst the Dead Sea scrolls (mss 4Q120).

[24] In the Greek, Ἐγένετο ἄνθρωπος, ἀπεσταλμένος παρὰ θεοῦ, ὄνομα αὐτῷ Ἰωάννης· (Technically in Greek it says, *name {given} to him: 'John'*.

[25] In Origenes' Greek: ...ἑρμηνεύεται γὰρ μετεωρισμὸς Ἰαώ 7, Τομος Β; *Commentary on the Gospel of John*.

[26] In Greek it is simply has the letter 'n' added plus a short ending, depending on the sentence ("ioann-es": Ἰωάνν-ης).

[27] GA 265, p. 215, (German edition).

[28] GA 267, p. 282, (German edition).

AD, he was never appointed as the senior church leader; never invited to participate as a prominent, indeed sanctified Elder. He was in fact by-passed by the officials of the newly established church. However, some more perceptive people did gather around him privately, for tuition about esoteric Christianity,

> After Lazaros-Johannes[29] came to Ephesus, he played no especial role {in the church}; {yet} he was one the most important persons {in the entire Christian world}. He had no special role in the administration of the church; instead other people were put in charge. When any such senior person died, someone else was chosen to replace him; without anyone thinking about having Lazaros-John placed at the head of the church...in the schooling-circle of Lazaros-Johannes, we are to see an especial community, who did not preach to the general mass of Christians. Indeed we know that the teachings of Lazaros-Johannes were regarded as dangerous for the general mass of Christians. It appears that with the schooling-circle of Lazaros-Johannes, we have to do with a kind of secret schooling-circle, a spiritual-esoteric community.[30]

This ignoring of such a great Christian initiate by church officials is all the more remarkable when one knows another comment from Rudolf Steiner concerning the words of Jesus, "Truly I say unto you, that some who are standing here, shall not taste death, before they see the kingdom of God." (Luke 9:27) Rudolf Steiner comments about this,

> This seeing of the kingdom of God occurs when the higher forces in the human soul arise into being. Lazaros-John experienced this...and from this, he wrote his Gospel...he had experienced what it actually, really, means to be a Christian.[31]

Two years later Rudolf Steiner commented,

> Lazaros-John[32] was the Disciple who was initiated, and who thus had the deepest things to communicate about the Christ-reality. Consequently the Gospel of John {Lazaros-John} is the deepest Gospel and also it has become a message {about Christ} to the explaining of which, there is no end. One can go ever deeper into it, and find ever new points; this is true, even for learned scholars.[33]

In terms of the social context of Lazaros, very little is known, other than that his sisters were the two women who have some prominence in the Gospels: Martha and Mary 'Magdalene'.[34] The only personal fact we know about Lazaros-John, is derived from Rudolf Steiner's research in the Akashic Record. Namely, that when he lived at Ephesus, he had a loyal and gifted student, who was a church elder. This man is known as John the Presbyter, who was not the same as St. John the Apostle. Nothing at all is known about this elder; but his name at least has survived in old church records.[35] Later, in the 13th century, Lazaros-John underwent an extraordinary initiation process, and became known thereafter as 'Christian Rosencreutz'. So, in viewing the painting of the Last Supper, as inspired into Leonardo, possibly by Christian Rosencreutz, we then also realize that the Last Supper event in AD 33 is a scene which occurred in the lifetime of Lazaros-John, and which deeply involves him.

---

[29] The manuscript has simply "John" as Rudolf Steiner did not reveal the facts about Lazaros as Lazaros-John, for several years.
[30] Archive lecture, *Christianity as Mystical Fact*, 4th April 1902.
[31] Archive lecture, *Christianity as Mystical Fact*, 15th Feb. 1902.
[32] The manuscript has simply "John" as Rudolf Steiner did not reveal the facts about Lazaros being Lazaros-John, for several years. I have used the term 'Lazaros-John here for clarity.
[33] Archive lecture, 25th July 1904.
[34] The theory that Lazaros-John was the son of a Boethus, a High Priest some 30 years earlier, is simply a theory, and it incorrectly assumes that Boethus had not only an Eleazar as a son, only a Martha as his daughter (which he did), but also a Mary (Magdalene), which he didn't. It also ignores the fact that, although 'Lazaros' can be a form of Eleazar, this was not the name ever used by Lazaros.
[35] Ref. 11: More about this man's role in the life of Lazaros-John will be explored in a future book specifically on the Gospel of John.

Lazaros: the Disciple whom the Lord loved

In the Gospel of John we find the expression, "the Disciple whom the Lord loved". Rudolf Steiner explains that, generally unknown to people in Christendom, there exists a secret, veiled aspect to Christianity. He explains that it was a requirement of world-destiny (or 'world-karma') that this religion would quickly lose its esoteric depth, and become an exoteric religion. This loss brought about a humanistic, earth-focussed way of thinking in Christendom, especially in the western world. As a result, it is virtually unknown today that hidden in the Gospels are profound and deeply sacred esoteric wisdom, or initiation truths. The rejection of the deeper, esoteric nature of the Christian truths, by the church resulted in a non-esoteric or more humanistic approach to the New Testament in academic-theological circles.

A comment by the prominent New Testament authority, Professor B. Metzger, on the determination in modern times to produce a modern English version of the Bible, reveals this tragic unawareness. The background to his comments are, that Bible scholars until about 1900 AD, had thought that God had especially created the type of Greek language used in the New Testament, since there were not many documents available in this everyday Greek. But about 1900 AD many old, sometimes fragmentary, non-religious Greek papyri, were discovered, written in the same kind of Greek of the Gospels, which showed theologians that this common Greek was the usual, everyday Greek of the times. These documents, he says,

> shed light on every aspect of life of the Greek-speaking people of the ancient world. It became clear that the New Testament documents were written in a plain, simple style to meet the needs of ordinary men and women. {Therefore,} Should they not be translated into the same kind of English? [36]

The correct answer to this question is of course, "no"; for a popular, 'flattened out' translation robs the text of its majestic and sacred deeper meaning, both the culturally obvious and the deeply hidden esoteric meaning. This attitude comes from precisely the tragic lack of spiritual-esoteric awareness in theological circles.[37] For although this language is a plainer Greek than that of Plato, it nevertheless has a complex grammatical structure to it, allowing veiled meanings to be conveyed. Even if for many, these deeper truths will remain hidden, the lofty ethical teachings would not be veiled from the "ordinary men and women", in a correctly nuanced, esoterically aware, translation. This mainstream attitude needs to give way to an esoteric approach to the Gospels, if the profoundly cosmic initiatory truths, the core significance of the Gospels, which are placed in the Gospels through a complex use of Greek, are to be communicated to people.

Our modern era, despite its materialistic trends, is an excellent time for this new approach to the Gospels to be undertaken, because of the pioneering and invaluable research by Rudolf Steiner. As he explains, this is when the reappearing to human consciousness of Jesus is occurring. That is, Jesus Christ is able to provide inspirational understanding to those who are seeking spirituality now, because people are starting to develop a slight awareness of the ethers (etheric clairvoyance); and hence some ability to receive, to intuit, spiritual wisdom from Jesus, which is being gently borne along in the ethers.[38]

The expression, "the Disciple whom the Lord loved" is an esoteric phrase, and means a follower of a Master who is the closest to him, in the esoteric sense: that is, the most deeply initiated.[39] In the case of Lazaros, this means that of the various apostles and followers, he was the closest to Christ; in Rudolf Steiner's words, his soul "had already been exposed to mighty influences

---

[36] B. Metzger, *The Bible in Translation*, p.103, Baker Academic, Michigan, 2001.

[37] This lack of awareness asserted itself as the proper, mature viewpoint, in the early 20th century; it is strongly present in the Bultmann school of theology, for example.

[38] For more about this, see my *Rudolf Steiner Handbook*.

[39] GA 94, p. 273, and GA 97, p.37: (pages numbers in the German editions).

from Jesus Christ".[40] What this means is quite remarkable: that Lazaros had been involved in a spiritual-initiatory process under the guidance of Jesus for some time, prior to him being "resurrected".[41] And a Scriptural reference actually confirms this, even though its significance has seldom been recognized. It precedes the miracle through which Lazaros is resurrected; his sisters send notice to Jesus, telling him that Lazaros is ill saying, "Lord, the one you love is sick." (John: 11; 3)

This expression, which is more accurately translated as "the one you are **fond of** is sick", tells us that Lazaros was already a person being mentored towards initiation by Jesus, and in fact was progressing in esoteric spiritual development. He would undergo the great, high point of initiation in the 'resurrection' event; and then he becomes the Disciple "whom Jesus loves". The event which enabled Lazaros to become such a holy person was the "raising of Lazaros" incident. Lazaros was already a highly evolved person due to his achievements in his past life, and had become the closest disciple of Christ. It is this prior development which enabled him to actually be initiated by Jesus himself. The famous 'raising of Lazaros' event, wherein he became the only person to be initiated by Jesus Christ, was a new version of the ancient classical three-day initiation 'sleep', which enabled Lazaros to attain the stage of the Spiritual-self, and even more than that, (as we shall see later). It is this process which made Lazaros into the Disciple "whom the Lord loved" (*agapeo*) and no longer just "fond of" (*phileo*). This is the final part of the event, as described in the Gospel of John,

> [Jn 11:40] Then Jesus said, "Did I not tell you that if you believed, you would see the glory of God?"
>
> [Jn 11:39] "Take away the stone," he said. "But, Lord," said Martha, the sister of the dead man, "by this time there is a bad odor, for he has been there four days."
>
> [Jn 11:40] Then Jesus said, "Did I not tell you that if you believed, you would see the glory of God?"
>
> [Jn 11:41] So they took away the stone. Then Jesus looked up and said, "Father, I thank you that you have heard me.
>
> [Jn 11:42] I knew that you always hear me, but I said this for the benefit of the people standing here, that they may believe that you sent me."
>
> [Jn 11:43] When he had said this, Jesus called in a loud voice, "Lazarus, come out!"
>
> [Jn 11:44] The dead man came out, his hands and feet wrapped with strips of linen and a cloth around his face. Jesus said to them, "Take off the grave clothes and let him go."

The involvement of Lazaros in the Last Supper

To understand where Lazaros-John is in the painting, which will take us into a deep esoteric-spiritual theme, we need to be aware of just how many clear, well-known 'facts' about Christianity are not really facts at all. For example, if we leave out the research of Rudolf Steiner, the year that Jesus was born in, is disputed; his birth-date is not agreed upon by New Testament scholars, even though we have our established Calendar of Year, with 1 BC-1AD. (Rudolf Steiner however, confirms that this Calendar is correct.) Secondly, it has remained a mystery as to when the Crucifixion and Resurrection of Christ actually happened – in what year it happened, in what the month remains unknown. (We noted above however, that Rudolf Steiner reveals it was in AD 33, from 3rd – 5th April; a date that agrees with the conclusions of a some theologians, and some academic researchers.[42])

The actual names of all the 12 disciples are unknown. No one can state just exactly who were the 12 Disciples, because the Gospel accounts of their names vary; but of course this inconsistency was smoothed out. Also, the lists of ancestors of Jesus in the Gospel of Luke

---

[40] GA 112, lecture, 1st July 1909.
[41] GA 112, lecture, 1st July 1909.
[42] C. Humphreys, *The Mystery of the Last Supper: reconstructing the final days of Jesus*, Cambridge Univ. Press, 2011.

varies totally from that of Matthew; no New Testament scholar has ever reconciled this bewildering fact, in a convincing way. (Rudolf Steiner has explained this, but that is not our theme here.) The Gospel of Matthew records Jesus riding into Jerusalem on Palm Sunday, on two donkeys simultaneously; it also records a man carrying a water-jar on his head, which socially, amongst the mainstream Jewish people would never happen. The list goes on and on. One cause of such remarkable inconsistencies or enigmas is that the Gospel writers had a specific intention of veiling deeply esoteric truths.

Now to our question: where is Lazaros-John in the painting? Is he that person on Jesus' right side, in a red over-garment and a dark blue tunic, who is being whispered to by St. Peter? It is generally understood that the Disciple there is the one "whom the Lord loveth"; but it is also understood that he is St. John, that is, John the Apostle, one of the 12 Disciples, the son of Zebedee, and brother of St. James. However, as we are about to discover, this is not the full reality. We also need to note that there is a rumour that this person on the right of Jesus is Mary Magdalene. As we shall soon see, this is a completely false theory, lacking both a sense of the sublime spiritual nature of Jesus Christ, as well as any intuitive sensing of the sacred initiatory secrets that lie behind the documents proclaiming Christianity. This figure, who is listening to St. Peter, and who is identified in the sketches by Leonardo, as "John", is identified by Rudolf Steiner as Lazaros-John. It is true that here he is given a feminine quality; the reason for this shall become clear quite soon.

From the indications of Rudolf Steiner, we can conclude that this delicate figure represents Lazaros-John, but, St. John the Apostle, one of the 12 Disciples, was also there. Many things – people and events – occurred in the life of Jesus which were connected to the activity of spiritual forces, and hence profoundly unusual. Rudolf Steiner explained that as an initiate, Lazaros-John was able to leave his body at will, and to **incorporate his soul (or astral body) into the aura of St. John the Apostle.**[43] This is not a difficult activity for someone who has been taken out of their body, in their initiatory three-day sleep event, which is what Lazaros experienced, enabling him to journey into spiritual realms. So John the Apostle was there, but so too was Lazaros-John, but in his astral body, not physically, even though Leonardo has depicted him as physically there.

Just how this dynamic was experienced by the eleven others around the table is unknown. Perhaps this kind of initiatory power, which merged the soul of Lazaros-John with the aura of the Apostle John, was cognized by the other Disciples; or perhaps they simply allowed this 'John' to behave in such a familiar way, and to be so close to Jesus, because Jesus himself was accepting of this. It is clear from Rudolf Steiner, that the Disciples were sometimes in a perplexed or dreamy state of mind, as they encountered the many extraordinary and sublime events wrought by Jesus, and especially so when faced with supernatural events. Their consciousness or ego-sense was at times hardly able to assimilate much of what they went through. One powerful example of this occurred when St. Peter was miraculously released from his chains inside a prison cell, by an Angel, and led out of the prison. St. Luke reports that St. Peter thought for a while that he was undergoing a kind of very real dream experience, as reported in the Book of Acts,

> Ac 12:7-9: Suddenly an angel of the Lord appeared and a light shone in the cell. He struck Peter on the side and woke him up. "Quick, get up!" he said, and the chains fell off Peter's wrists. Then the angel said to him, "Put on your clothes and sandals." And Peter did so. "Wrap your cloak around you and follow me," the angel told him.
> Peter followed him out of the prison, but he had no idea that what the angel was doing was really, actually happening; he thought he was seeing a vision.

---

[43] Spoken in answer to a question from two of the founding priests of the Christian Community church, Bock and Klein; reported in GA 264, p. 239.

So, what Rudolf Steiner is revealing is that at the Last Supper, **both** men were present; one physically, the other in his astral body. But the narrative in the Gospel, and in the composition of the painting by Leonardo, focuses upon Lazaros-John's presence there. This focus on 'the beloved disciple' creates a situation which presents in a profound way the spiritual dynamics occurring in the event, as we shall see when we analyse the figures in the painting. Before we start to assess the painting in detail, we need to be clear about the cosmic or divine beings associated with Jesus, and which form a core aspect of the painting about the Last Supper.

A cosmic Christianity

At this point, we need to become familiar with Christianity as understood through the high initiation capacities of Rudolf Steiner, because the Last Supper painting has a number of profound meanings which are derived from initiation knowledge. We noted earlier that Rudolf Steiner taught a 'cosmic' Christianity, and we have seen that the Gospel of John commences on a lofty note, referring to "the Logos". The Logos is mentioned by Rudolf Steiner, in many lectures, as a sublime deity who over-shadowed Jesus, as from the Baptism of Jesus by John the Baptist in the Jordan River. His explanation is from the context of a very living and complex cosmos, wherein – in spiritual realms, far above the physical-mineral world – nine ranks of divine beings exist. This Logos is an alternative name for the 'cosmic' Christ – meaning here a divine being, not the man, Jesus. The Greek word 'Logos' was used by people in the initiatory schools of the Hellenistic Age to mean a high spiritual being whom we could define in general terms, as the 'Soul of the Cosmos', or in modern terms, the high spiritual Intelligence behind Creation. The initiate Heraclitus, who was writing about 500 BC, conveys a good idea of what the esoteric Greek understanding of the Logos was. Heraclitus writes for example,

> "Although this Logos is eternally valid, yet people are unable to understand it….although all things come to pass in accordance with this Logos, yet people seem to be quite without any experience of it...
> Although intimately connected with the Logos which orders the whole world, men keep setting themselves against it, and the things which they encounter every day seem quite foreign to them." (Saying 1 & 64) [44]

But the ancient Greeks could refer to many kinds of spiritual energies resounding through the cosmos to the inner ear of the old seers, as 'a logos', or in the plural as various 'logoi'. However, in these usages, it would simply mean a spiritual-astral resonance, whereas in John's Gospel, and with an initiate like Heraclitos, the word 'logos' refers to a real being. That it was used in the Gospel of John indicates that the gospel was designed to be a meditative text for those with a more esoteric approach to Christianity.

The nine ranks of divine beings

The nine ranks of divine beings each has a specific area of the solar system where they normally manifest (on a spiritual level). In terms of these nine ranks of divine beings, the Logos or cosmic Christ, is the highest of the 'Powers', as St Paul calls them. Now, the Powers are associated with the sun; so they are in effect, sun gods. There are seven of these beings; and the highest of these Powers is the being referred to as the cosmic Christ, in anthroposophy. This deity can also be called the 'solar Logos', see illustration 3. The Powers are of the same rank as the beings known in the Old Testament (in Hebrew) as the 'Elohim'. One of these Powers is known as 'Jehovah', who is the primary deity of the Old Testament. But at times Jehovah represents all of these Powers, especially the highest, the cosmic Christ,

However, and this might seem complex, but it is not really difficult, Rudolf Steiner explains that 'the Logos' is a term that can be applied to **two deities**, both of whom are referred to as "Christ". This other Logos is a much higher being than even the highest of the Powers, in glory and in

---

[44] On the internet the Complete Fragments of Heraclitus are available.

spiritual evolution. This other 'Logos' is above all of the nine ranks of beings; it is part of the primal Trinity, or three-fold Godhead.

These nine ranks of beings, and their associated planetary spheres, are:

Angels: in the Moon sphere, helping human beings to develop the Spiritual-self
Archangels: in the Venus sphere, helping human beings to develop the Life-spirit
Principalities: in the Mercury sphere, helping human beings to develop the Spirit-human (Atma)

Powers: in the Sun sphere: one of these is Jahve, but the highest is the Christ or solar Logos
Mights: in the Mars sphere
Dominions: in the Jupiter sphere

Thrones: in the Saturn sphere
Cherubine: in the outer areas of the solar system
Seraphine: over-seeing the solar system; receptive to the will of the (zodiacal) Logos

Illustration 3 shows the spheres of these beings in the solar system and the location of the two great deities referred to as a Logos.

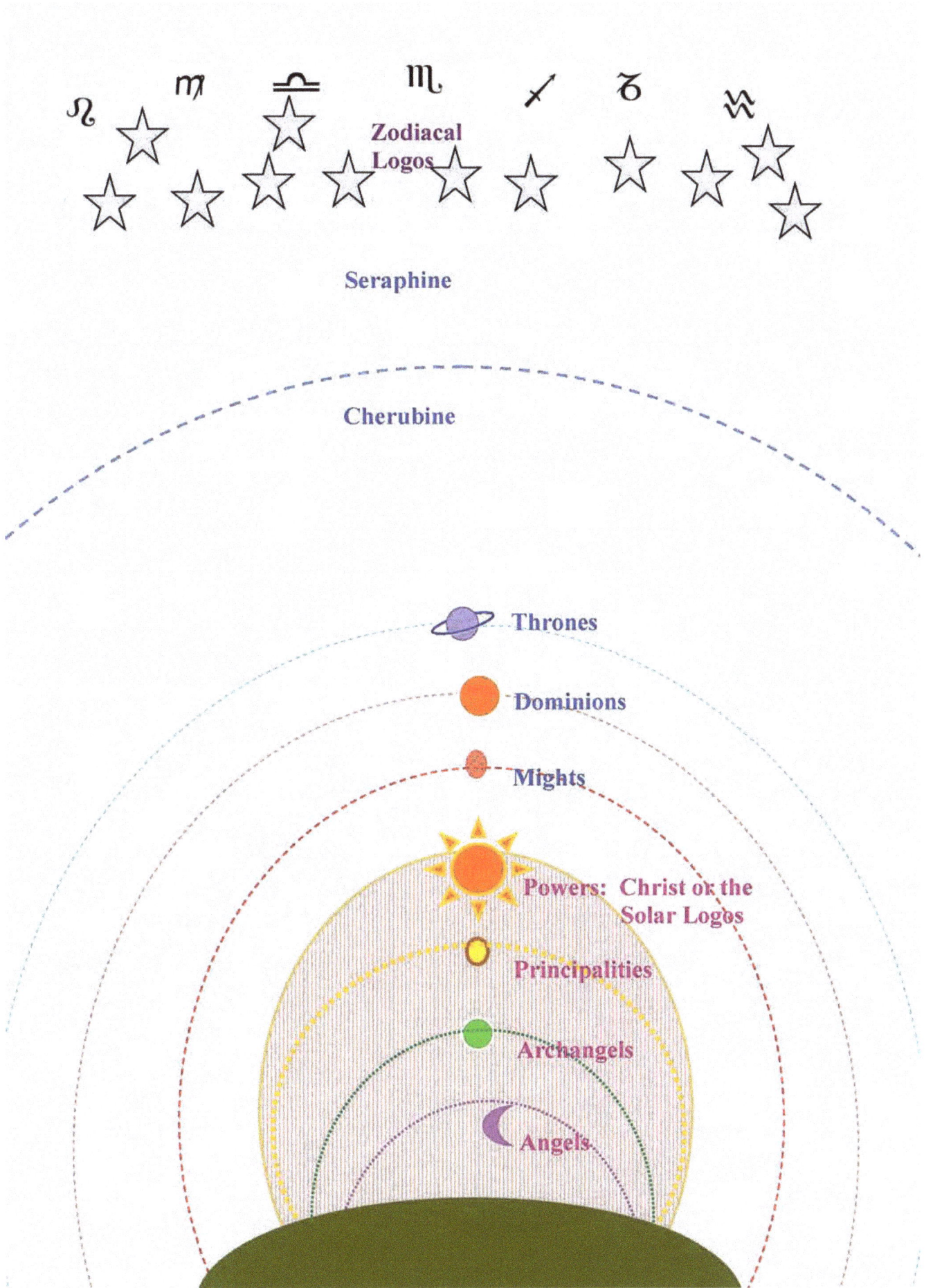

3 The relation of the Solar Logos and the Zodiacal Logos to the nine ranks of divine beings.

The zodiacal Logos: a sublime deity who created the Zodiac

So, the term Logos was also applied to a much higher deity than the sun-god Christ (the solar Logos); namely to a sublime being from whom creation itself arose, in response to the will of the Father-god. This deity could be called the 'zodiacal Logos', because this god brought the zodiac system into existence. An ancient text about this sublime being is found in the so-called Gospel of Truth, an esoteric text written about 100 AD, included in the collection of ancient texts found in Egypt (in Nag Hammadi). It was written only a few decades after the Gospel of John,

> The Logos, the Word of the Father God, rays forth into the world as the fruit of His heart and as the expression of his will. (V.23)[45]

To understand the real depths of the Last Supper, we need to be aware of these two Logos beings. There is a wonderful, artistic way to contemplate these deep mysteries in a pastel drawing by Rudolf Steiner which is specifically illustrating the events on Golgotha, as the cosmic Christ and the zodiacal Logos descend to the Earth.

Pastel drawing of the Golgotha event

In this pastel drawing, we see Golgotha hill, in a brown colouring, where Jesus is being crucified, along with two other men; see illustration 4.

They are enshrouded in the mysterious darkness which occurred as Jesus hung on the cross. Inside the earth, in black, is the figure of Ahriman; above him is the sun-god Christ, (or solar Logos) a huge, somewhat human-like figure in a golden colour. Spiritual forces are raying downwards from his right hand, causing Ahriman to be isolated deep inside the Earth. The left hand of the sun-god is raised upwards, and above it, enveloped in a bright red colour, is the figure of Lucifer, who is now surrounded by a radiant cloud of golden light. Lucifer is a term used for the fallen Power who has triggered off the sense of self in the soul long ages ago, through stimulating a capacity for thinking and experiencing sensual desires. It is this process which is behind what is known as the 'Fall of Man'. The term Ahriman refers to a fallen Power who is fully evil, and a subtle part of his influence on the human soul brings about a materialistic way of thinking as well as cold, anti-social will.

In the drawing, Lucifer is being caught up in the process of losing his power, a painful process which however, is the prelude to his redemption. Above Lucifer is the moon, signifying that Lucifer went through his 'fall' in the Moon aeon. The same scene is depicted by Rudolf Steiner in the magnificent wooden sculpture, called the Group, where more details are shown than here in this pastel drawing. In his comments on the carving of this theme, Rudolf Steiner informs us that Christ did not exert any compulsion against Lucifer, but rather that Lucifer himself, from within, was ethically 'over-thrown' by the near presence of divine goodness. Ahriman however, was specifically sought out and sent deep into the Earth's interior, in a weakened state.

But to the left side of the drawing, from high up in heavenly realms, a beautiful, shining yellow-white light is descending downwards, to Jerusalem. This celestial cascade of light, the second of the two divine realities in the drawing, appears to represent the zodiacal Logos.

---

[45] The Gospel of Truth, The Nag Hammadi Library in English, Leiden, 1977, Brill.

4 Rudolf Steiner's depiction of the Golgotha event.

The zodiacal Logos and the solar Logos were both over-shadowing Jesus

The general understanding and feeling, in exoteric Christianity, that Jesus 'was divine', becomes raised to lofty heights through Rudolf Steiner's profound esoteric teaching as to what the Christ-impulse is, in reality. The broad term, 'divine', or the very vague term, 'God', becomes imbued with real clarity, allowing us to have a much more specific, and therefore a much clearer, understanding. It is a central theme in anthroposophy that the 'Christ' is the highest of the sun-gods; this Being can also be called the 'solar Logos', as we have noted earlier. There are many references to this divinity in the works of Rudolf Steiner, where the sun-gods are identified with 'the Elohim', mentioned in the Hebrew text of the book of Genesis. These are the beings who "created Heaven and Earth", but in translation are referred to as a single deity, God. In one of his references to Christ as the highest of the sun-gods, Rudolf Steiner comments,

> But the leader of all of the other beings, who unfold their beneficial activity from the sun, down towards the Earth, is that being who was later called "Christ".[46]

In his lecture cycles on the Gospel of John, Rudolf Steiner emphasizes the 'Christ-being' who united to the Earth's aura, was the great sun-god, or 'solar Logos'; the highest of the seven Powers or sun gods.[47] But also, on just a few occasions, Rudolf Steiner mentioned that there is a second 'Logos' or 'Christ'. In my work on the Greek texts of a third century church Father, Origenes of Alexandria, I made a major discovery in relation to what Origenes taught regarding the cosmic aspect of Christianity. Here Origenes teaches a doctrine that is supportive of Rudolf Steiner's teachings. He taught that there are **two** cosmic 'Christ' beings; although this is not known in the academic world generally. In his commentary on the Gospel of John, this great Christian teacher actually identifies 'Christ', whom he calls the Logos, as the leader of "the Hosts of Yahweh-Sabaoth"; this little-known Hebrew term appears in English as "The Lord of Hosts". It is clear from anthroposophical knowledge that these beings are called by St. Paul 'Powers', and these deities have their manifestation in the spiritual sun; so they are 'sun-gods'.

However, Origenes also indicates that the term "Christ" is the title for another being who is also referred to as 'Logos': namely that Logos-being who is mentioned in the prologue to the Gospel of John. This second deity is understood in anthroposophy as the 'zodiacal Logos', so a being far beyond the Powers. This primordial Logos is a much higher spiritual being than the other 'Christ'. But both of these high spiritual beings became part of the Earth's aura through the events on Golgotha: this is the core teaching from Rudolf Steiner about the meaning of the events on Golgotha. The deeper meaning of the painting by Leonardo cannot be discovered if one does not know about the primal Logos, from whom the zodiac derives.

Origenes has been writing about the Logos, whom he presents as the primal wisdom of God, because he believes that this Logos being is inspired from the sublime wisdom of the 'Welten grund' or primal Father God. It is after mentioning this primal Logos that he continues on to mention that the 'Christ' or 'the Logos' is also, in another aspect, a high spiritual being – the highest of the Hosts of the Yahweh-Sabaoth, who is associated with a rank of spiritual beings who are not as high as the zodiacal Logos. Let's see the first part of this text; it is a bit difficult. This is because it is a slightly condensed version, copied by a courageous, unknown monk when the works of Origenes were being aggressively destroyed by later Church Fathers. But it is the only text left in the entire Christian world to preserve knowledge of this two-fold cosmic nature of Christ; so it is worthwhile grappling with it,

> And further, for the clear understanding of the {**other** aspect of Christ, separate from the zodiacal} Logos, having its own defined separate individuality (περιγραφην), of the kind attaining to life in itself, one must speak about Powers, not only power. Frequently it is

---

[46] GA 114, lecture, 21st Sept., 1909.

[47] One of these seven is Jahve, or Jehovah, whose place of manifestation is the moon; GA103, lecture, 26th May, 1908.

set forth {in Scripture} "For thus says the Lord of the Powers": {this phrase refers to} certain divine, living beings, with high consciousness, {who are} designated "Powers" – of whom Christ was the highest and the finest, {thusly} being called not only the 'wisdom of God' but also 'the power (of God)'.[48]

In other words, 'Christ' here means the highest of the sun-gods, the Powers, or what in anthroposophical knowledge are called the Spirits of Form. Having written this extraordinary passage, saying that the Christ (as a member of the hierarchies) is unique, in that he is the highest of his particular rank of beings, Origenes continues, referring back to the zodiacal Logos. He explains that this primal, sublime Logos (the World-Soul of Heraclitos) is also unique, because even though it is so sublimely great that it is beyond the state of an individualized entity, it is nevertheless a quite definite specific entity. This somewhat contradictory statement is how Origenes explains that the zodiacal Logos is not just one of the many diffuse, cosmic energies or 'cosmic words' which stream through the cosmos, for it does have a real being-ness, but it is so high above what our consciousness can grasp, that the concept of being individualized does not seem to apply;

> **Therefore, just as** numerous mighty Spirit-Hosts of God exist (*the Powers*), each one of whom has individualization, yet all of whom are excelled by the Saviour {Christ within this hierarchy of beings} – **so too** even if the {primal zodiacal} Logos...is not individualized anywhere, outside us[49] – this {primal Logos-}'Christ' will be understood, through our elucidations in previous pages, as having real being-ness in Wisdom, in the Beginning {of creation}.[50]

So, there is another 'Christ' or Logos, who is part of the primal Trinity, far beyond the nine ranks of hierarchical beings; and indeed so far beyond, that the human mind cannot think of this deity as having a specific, individualized nature. The reason for this situation is **that all of Creation is this being**. So when this ancient text is correctly translated, it reveals this early church Father is identifying 'Christ' as A: the highest of the Powers of sun-gods, and B: as the sublime Logos, beyond the hierarchies; that is, the zodiacal Logos. Later we shall consider the intriguing reference by Origenes about the zodiacal Logos being 'individualized within humanity'. Here we shall just note that this theme closely relates to the painting by Leonardo, in that the Disciples each are a kind of embodiment of the Logos, for they have a link to the zodiac. This is a topic which we shall be exploring in detail later.

Actually, Rudolf Steiner's references to the great zodiacal Logos are in fact fewer, and less detailed, than the references to the solar Logos. In these references he does teach that the divine aspect of Jesus extends beyond that of the solar Logos, up to the zodiacal Logos. So it would be helpful now if we note some statements from Rudolf Steiner about a 'cosmic Christ-impulse', which includes the zodiacal Logos merging with Jesus and thus being brought into the Earth-soul, at the Crucifixion. As we do this, we just need to bear in mind that the sparkling, golden-white ray descending in the pastel drawing can be understood as representing the zodiacal Logos, whilst the towering golden figure represents the solar logos. One can only wonder at, and yearn for, the rich spiritual wisdom that was once present in what we now have left as the Christian religion.

---

[48] For those who know Greek, confusion is possible here, as the term dunameis is used, which later designated a specific rank of hierarchical spirit being. But in the Septuagint, and in this passage from Origenes, it simply has the nuance of powerful or mighty (to translate the Hebrew term, Jahveh-Sabaoth). The rank of beings involved is 'the Powers'.

[49] In Origenes' Greek: οὗτος καὶ λόγος εἰ καὶ ὁ παρ' ἡμῖν οὐκ ἔστι κατά περιγραφήν, ἐκτός ἡμιν..

[50] It is the interconnected and underlined apparently minor phrases "just as therefore (mighty) ....so too (the Logos).... [Ὥσπερ οὖν δυνάμεις Θεοῦ .... οὗτος καὶ λόγος] which are contrasting the two beings, that have not been given their essential weight by the two earlier English translations of this text (R. Heine & A. Menzies).

The Zodiacal Logos

Rudolf Steiner seldom referred to the zodiacal Logos, perhaps because such a concept was too esoteric, or too large a step to take, for his audiences at that time. But we can now encounter some of his statements, sprinkled thought his 354 books, which confirm that the 'Christ-being' or 'Christ-impulse' which was, in various ways, united with Jesus, or over-shadowing him, does encompass the great, primordial, zodiacal Logos. And since this second, sublime god is implicit in the Last Supper, we need to be clear about this,

> Gift upon gift humanity received, in order to further develop its nature on all sides, and to thereby become mature enough to receive the highest of its {*spiritual*} potential, from the Christ, when he descended down to the Earth, and incarnated into Jesus of Nazareth. Christ is so mighty a being that even for the highest clairvoyant consciousness, he remains unfathomable. No matter how high an initiate may raise his or her vision, he or she can comprehend only a negligible part of this being.[51]

It is clear that that a high Initiate can fully perceive the sun-gods, who are known as the Powers; so these words are referring to a much higher being. On another occasion, when he was speaking of the significance of the events at Golgotha, and these were heralded by the Last Supper, Rudolf Steiner clarified this further,

> However, the Christ within his own specific being, is not, so to speak, contained within the sheaths of Jesus of Nazareth {*that is, his physical, etheric and astral bodies*}. Rather he is the leader and guide of all the higher Hierarchies {*from the Angels, through the Powers, up to the Seraphim*}. He is an all-encompassing, cosmic, universal Being; and just as, through the Mystery of Golgotha, he entered into the flow of human evolving, so too were there consequences of this for the beings of these higher hierarchies....[52]

These statements are in effect saying that 'the Christ' meant here is in fact the zodiacal Logos; that is, that sublime being whose intentions underlie the creative activity of the all hierarchical beings. It also indicates that this sublime being, who transcends the 'God' of the book of Genesis, (that is, the Sun gods or Powers) was not within the 'sheaths' of Jesus, but was above him, but linked through a presence it has **within the sun god**. That the zodiacal Logos was present within the high sun-god Christ, or the solar Logos, was also indicated in a lecture in 1922, when Rudolf Steiner told his audience that,

> The Christ – who today is known as the being who went through the Mystery of Golgotha at the beginning of the Christian era – this 'Christ' descended from out of still higher regions down to the Sun (long ages before the events in Palestine); there Zarathustra beheld him.[53]

Normally Rudolf Steiner in reference to Zarathustra taught that he saw the high sun-god Christ, (the solar Logos); but here we are given a further glimpse of the colossal fact that within the sun-god Christ there was present an aspect of the great primordial Logos, the zodiacal Logos. A meditative indication as to how high in spiritual rank this zodiacal Logos is, can be obtained from notes taken from a question and answer session, after a lecture on Easter Sunday of 1913, where Rudolf Steiner had been speaking about the cosmic Christ coming to the Earth,

> The Physical body of Christ is the Sun
> The Etheric body of Christ are the seven planets
> The astral body of Christ is the zodiac
> The ego of Christ is entirely beyond even the Zodiac [54]

---

[51] GA 118, lecture, 13th April 1910.
[52] GA 129, lecture, 21st Aug. 1911.
[53] GA 211, lecture, 24th April, 1922, London..
[54] GA 150, editor's end-note #35 p.138.

There are various extraordinary revelations here about the nature of the sublime zodiacal Logos, with some complex implications. What is important is, as we noted above, that the Logos had created the zodiac; but here we learn that it was from out of what we would understand, in human terms, his 'astral body' or soul. In other words, the entire cosmic arrangement which we call 'the zodiac' was brought about by the Logos, yet it was not created from the very highest aspect of this being's nature.

To be more specific about the Idea of the zodiac, one could say that through mighty 'imaginative thoughts', during an ancient past evolutionary phase of the Earth's evolution, the Logos prepared a special positioning of the future Earth, in its orbiting, relative to the Sun in the cosmos. This special position would be such that the people on the Earth would experience the sun as passing in front of a selection of twelve specific star groupings, which we today call the zodiac. These zodiacal stars groupings or constellations, spatially viewed, are themselves dispersed throughout our galaxy; some are near, others are further away from our solar system, but nevertheless the sun in its motions, as viewed from the Earth, passes 'through' them.

Consequently in a more private esoteric group, Rudolf Steiner told his students that the words in the Gospel of John, "In the beginning was the Word..." refers to the zodiacal logos. He explains that even before the Saturn aeon began, the Logos, as the great 'Creative Word', was sending forth its creative intentions into the cosmos. And he then comments that as result of this process, we human beings have a zodiacal element in us; we are a kind of microcosm of the zodiac. Therefore, when the Earth aeon has run its course, we human beings shall have become beings who speak forth the zodiacal cosmos, creatively. [55]

The cosmic Christ and Jesus in the Gospel of Lazaros-John

The report about the Last Supper in John's Gospel occupies five chapters, whereas the report in Mark's Gospel occupies just eight verses, and Matthew uses thirteen verses. John's report culminates in the 17th chapter, with the 'Prayer of the High Priest', wherein a truly startling passage occurs. An esoteric deepening of one's understanding of the four Gospels, through Rudolf Steiner, lets one understand that when Jesus speaks, an inherently unified being, 'Jesus-Christ', is speaking, wherein deity and sanctified human are as one. But in addition, Rudolf Steiner taught that sometimes, the cosmic Christ Itself is speaking through Jesus, as a more specifically, more separate being, as it were, than at other times.

We have already noted one of these occasions in the Gospel of John, when the cosmic Christ directly spoke, describing himself (or Itself) as the "light of the world"; as the sun-god or Power, from the sun-sphere. But in the address given at the Last Supper, in Chapter 17, there is an even more startling occasion. This majestic, profound chapter, in Verse two, has statements about how it is God's intention, through Christ, that people receive "eternal life".

This famous term is more understandable, and more accurately translated as 'aeonic existence'. In other words, this phrase actually means that after death, human beings may have conscious existence (or 'life') in the divine worlds (called 'the aeons' in Hellenistic times). Then in Verse three, words occur which have really perplexed theologians down through the centuries, as they are truly startling, and for which they could not find a satisfactory explanation,

> In the NIV version:
> John 17:3 Now this is eternal life: that they may know you the only true God, and Jesus Christ, whom you have sent.

---

[55] GA 266-1, p. 209.

In my translation:

And this is aeonic existence: namely that they cognize You (*as*) the only true God, and {that they cognize} Jesus, the Messiah, (*as*) the one whom You sent forth {to humanity}.[56]

It really seems that here Jesus is referring to himself **by his own name** ! In most translations the name "Jesus Christ" does occur, (as here in the NIV), although I have used the expression, "Jesus, the Messiah" (which means, 'the Anointed One'), because the Aramaic equivalent of this phrase was used in Palestine and beyond, and would have been used of Jesus by his contemporaries who were discussing him. Only gradually, as the Gospel message was spread via the Greek language, was the Greek term "Christ" used to mean 'Anointed One' or 'Messiah'.

Over some decades this expression, "Jesus, the Anointed One" (the Messiah), became fixed into a kind of set name, "Jesus Christ", like 'John Smith'. But these words in the Gospel were spoken before that happened. So in this passage from the Gospel, I myself and various theologians, view the term, "Jesus, the Messiah" as the correct translation, because the famous term, or name, "Jesus Christ" had not yet historically come into being. This only happened decades later, when the Christian religion was forming.

So, here we have the speaker naming a person called Jesus, who is defined as the Messiah, therefore one may conclude that the speaker in this verse **is not Jesus**, because a person does not normally refer to themselves by their own name. Scholars are perplexed by this sentence; some have suggested that these words come from the writer of the Gospel, and **not from Jesus**. For example, the Reverend Plummer concludes that these words are "not without difficulty", but are an insertion from the Gospel writer. Professor Godet concludes that here Jesus felt he should "state clearly for once that he is the Messiah, before he dies". Professor B. F. Westcott observes that these words "present a great difficulty", and remain a puzzle. Professor T. Zahn concludes that Jesus is here educating his listeners (readers) as to how to understand, and thus address him, once the church has been formed.

Professor Dr. Prelate Pölzl argued for the convoluted idea that Jesus, as part of God, sets himself aside from God in this instance to require that people "cognise God and himself (as part of God) as objects to be cognized"… in order to achieve eternal life. (See Appendix One for more details of various scholars' interpretation of this sentence). To explore the profound theme here of 'cognizing God' would take us into a very complex discussion, requiring many pages; so that shall be explored in another book. But we can see that theologians cannot understand what is happening here.

In contrast to their thoughts, I have concluded from a study of the Greek text, and from Rudolf Steiner's comments on this passage, that the speaker is the sun-god, the "cosmic Christ", (understood as being present within Jesus). In his comments on this verse, Rudolf Steiner speaks about our sense of "I" in relation to God, and tells his audience that the Mystery of Golgotha comes as a new element to this age-old dynamic. He explains how here in this passage, people are being informed (by the cosmic Christ) that humanity now needs to feel, in freedom, the 'Son-God' in relation to their innermost "I" (meaning the sun-god, 'Christ'), and not only the 'Father-God', which humanity in the old religions had been doing for millennia.

So what we actually have here is a passage **wherein 'the cosmic Christ' is speaking, and who names Jesus as the Messiah.** A divine being is declaring that to attain an empowered consciousness in divine realms (to have 'eternal life'), human beings need to have some inner unity with, or intuitive awareness of, the spiritual reality, or God; and they also need an awareness of Jesus as the Messiah, as the vessel of God. The word "God" here we could understand as referring to the Father-God; that is, a being who is higher than the cosmic Christ.

---

[56] The Greek here is: αὕτη δέ ἐστιν ἡ αἰώνιος ζωὴ ἵνα γινώσκωσιν σὲ τὸν μόνον ἀληθινὸν θεὸν καὶ ὃν ἀπέστειλας Ἰησοῦν Χριστόν

The term 'God' is, as Rudolf Steiner explains, a term that directs people's minds and hearts to the Divine; but it is not a specific, precise term. For example, in terms of the Book of Genesis, where the first sentence says, "In the beginning God created Heaven and Earth", the deity meant there is the highest of the Powers or sun-gods, that is, Christ. But in terms of many Gospel references, it refers to the highest of the sublime Thrones; and there are other, even higher meanings in the Gospels.

So, it is with these astonishing, awe-inspiring words in the 17th Chapter, proclaiming a cosmic Christianity, that Lazaros-John brings to an end his account of the Last Supper, thereby alerting the reader who has esoteric awareness, that very soon a colossal cosmic drama will be enacted, **a drama involving sublime deities**, once Jesus is arrested and the sacrifice on Golgotha hill occurs. The sheer holiness and majesty of this 17th chapter is derived from its presenting of deep cosmic truths about the Christ-reality on an initiatory level. And it is this sense of holiness and cosmic drama that has imbued the painting with its power.

So, on a deeper level, the events of Golgotha which led to the development of the Christian religion, consisted of processes unknown to Christian theologians, for this religion lost its esoteric core after just a few centuries. The Golgotha events resulted in the Earth's aura and its life-forces becoming imbued with the light, with the spiritual powers, of two high spiritual beings: the solar Logos and the zodiacal Logos. This occurred through the sacrifice made by Jesus Christ; a sacrificial intention arising from a divine love. These cosmic events, on Golgotha hill have given the possibility to human beings through the intermediary role of Jesus, to develop their spiritual potential. In anthroposophical wisdom, this potential has three distinct aspects to it. There is the 'Spiritual-self' which arises when the soul is ennobled; and there is also our Life-spirit, which arises from the spiritualization of our etheric body or life-energies after the soul or astral body has been ennobled. This second spiritual element bestows the capacity to create beauty, and harmony and healing, on various levels. Thirdly, there is the mysterious Spirit-human, which arises when the subconscious will forces underlying the body are ennobled; we shall consider this in more detail, later.

The Last Supper painting obviously portrays a crucial moment when Judas is to be identified, and as such, the painting – in its most obvious meaning – is about the sacrifice of Jesus and the role of evil in the world. But in addition, the Last Supper painting has many veiled meanings which communicate secrets of esoteric Christianity; truths which give understanding of the deep link that exists between the Logos and the zodiac, and Jesus with his Disciples. In this book, we shall be going through a process of contemplating the zodiac implications of the Last Supper painting, step by step, using extracts from an extraordinary unpublished archive document which specifically explains the link between the Disciples and the zodiac. But we shall start with identifying the 12 Disciples, and learning a little about them. Then we shall explore the obvious level of meaning of the painting, which is to do with Judas and evil. First we need to contemplate the emotional responses of the Disciples as portrayed in the great painting.

5 Identifying the Disciples in the painting.

Bartholomew / James-Less /Andrew   Judas / Peter /Lazaros   Thomas /James-Grt. /Philip   Matthew / Jude / Simon Zelotes

Chapter Three: Encountering the 12 Disciples

The soul gestures of the 12 Disciples
(from left to right)

The body language of the twelve is very expressive, and here I am putting forward my own interpretation of these gestures.

Bartholomew:	He is indignant, leaps to the defence of Christ
James the Less:	Supporting Peter's action of asking the question
Andrew:	Displaying shock and horror
Judas Iscariot:	Appears alarmed that his plans are known to Jesus
Peter:	He is asking Lazaros to enquire whom it is
Lazaros-John:	A gesture here of innocence, of non-involvement
Thomas:	Displaying doubt, true to his nature
James the Great:	Deep shock, and disbelief
Philip:	Imploring: hoping that this is not true
Matthew:	Asking Simon whether this could possibly be true
Jude:	Asking Simon if it is true, does he have any idea who it is
Simon Zelotes:	He is bewildered

It is doubtful that one can accurately associate these gestures and reactions to the various zodiacal signs or to the zodiacal correlation of eurythmy gestures. (Eurythmy is a new art of dance or movement, inaugurated by Rudolf Steiner which makes visible the cosmic forces in speech and music.)

Judas' response perhaps could be expanded from the historical perspective, not the esoteric viewpoint: "*Could it be my strategy that he is calling treason?*" Judas was money hungry, but this additional sentence is based on the widely held view that Judas, by assisting the Sanhedrin to arrest Jesus, was, in his own mind, trying to force the hand of Jesus, to assert himself over the political situation and thereby establish an earthly kingdom. Also Judas' greed may have been enticed by the thought that power and wealth would be his, in the new earthly 'Kingdom'.

Notice too, how the shock-wave that emerged from the words of Jesus has spread out to his left and right, but now is re-bounding back toward Jesus. On his right, Bartholomew has jumped to his feet and sending it back to the centre, so to speak, and likewise on the left of Jesus, Simon Zelotes and Matthew's hand gestures both point back towards the centre.

Some notes about each disciple: in the sequence as shown in the painting
(from left to right)

With some of the Disciples, there is no historically verified knowledge about their biography at all. It is also not possible to know just who some of the Disciples were, in terms of another Biblical person who has the same name. The following information is an attempt to present what is known of these Disciples, according to verifiable information, as well as some of the more reliable statements which have been preserved in the historical traditions of various churches. But what is regarded as correct according to one very early church record, which often was not written down for a century or longer, can contradict the viewpoint maintained by a church in another country.

However, in terms of the spiritual research of Rudolf Steiner, the past karma of the 12 Disciples can be known, to some extent. In his lectures on the Gospel of St. Mark, Rudolf Steiner refers his listeners to the historical events recorded in two writings contained in the Apocrypha: *Maccabees 1* and *Maccabees 2*. These writings elaborate on the battle for the spiritual integrity of Israel in the two centuries prior to the Christian era, in the course of a revolt against the Seleucid Empire. Five sons of a high priest called Mattathias, became prominent in this time as defenders of Israel; one of these, Judas Maccabee, became especially prominent as a guerrilla leader against the Grecian Seleucid army.

Eventually, in 161 BC, this Judas made a contract with the Roman authorities in his fight against the Seleucids. But this deal had the terrible consequence that eventually the Romans, through Pompey, annexed Syria and became the rulers of Judea, entering Jerusalem in 63 BC. Also in this turbulent time, partly historical, partly legendary records relate that seven Maccabean men stood up against the Seleucid ruler and were cruelly martyred as a consequence. Rudolf Steiner confirms these reports as reflecting actual historical events. He informed his audience that these 12 men, the five sons of Mattathias and the seven Maccabean men appeared again, (about 140 years later) as the 12 Disciples.

What is particularly striking is that the extreme rebel, Judas Maccabees, became Judas Iscariot. So, he is a valid part of the 12-fold circle of helpers of the Christ, but he has some substantial imperfections. He had an inappropriate driving force which led to the political deal-making that was harmful to the interests of his own people. As a brief further point to the karmic biography of Judas, Rudolf Steiner taught that Judas Iscariot, in his next life became a prominent theologian, working in the Roman church. The Roman church both provided a substantial framework for the spread of Christianity, but also interwove into this a quality which was non-esoteric, and indeed antagonistic to the cosmic esoteric truths of Christianity.

The Disciples, with their names as listed here, is what was written by Leonardo in his own notebooks; these were published in 1955, in *The Notebooks of Leonardo Da Vinci.*
When 'church tradition' is noted below, this refers to the historical views of various churches, including the Assyrian, Iranian, Greek, Roman and Armenian.

BARTHOLOMEW
He was born at Cana.
Almost nothing else is known about him.
In the church tradition:
He probably went to Armenia, after preaching in Asia Minor.
Death: he might have been martyred in AD 68 in Azerbaijan.
Tomb: near Baskale, in Turkey: many alleged pieces of his body are venerated in various churches.

He might be the Disciple also called Nathanael, since Bartholomew is never mentioned in John's Gospel, and Nathanael is never mentioned in the other three Gospels, it is quite possible that these two names refer to the same person. This 'double name' situation also applies to 'Simon-Peter', 'Mathew-Levi', and 'Jude-Thaddeus', and Lazaros-John.

If Nathanael is a separate person to Bartholomew, then, like Lazaros-John, he is a very important follower of Jesus who is not, apparently, in the group of 12 Disciples. Rudolf Steiner refers to Nathanael as a "fifth degree initiate" and as such someone who was able to commune with the archangelic Folk-spirit of his nation, Israel.

JAMES son of Alphaeus

Nothing is known of this James.

There are many people called 'James' in the New Testament, and this causes great confusion in historical research. He might be an Apostle called, "James the Less".

He might also be the same person as "James the Younger".

Death: unknown

Tomb: unknown

ANDREW

He was born in Galilee, probably at Bethsaida.

He had earlier followed John the Baptist.

When the Baptist referred to Jesus as the Lamb of God, Andrew and another Disciple, set out to meet Jesus; from this meeting he became a Disciple (John 1:35-39).

Andrew introduced Peter his brother, and also Philip, to Jesus.

He is prominent as the scribe for the esoteric-Gnostic teachings of the Risen Saviour, in the ancient Coptic Gnostic text, *Pistis Sophia.*

According to the early church historian Eusebius, and ancient Greek tradition, Andrew preached in Southern Russia, as far as the Caspian Sea, and then in Istanbul; he also preached near Ephesus, in Asia Minor.

Death: Greek tradition states that he was martyred in the town of Patras.

Tomb: in Patras is a reliquary with his head; it is believed that some bones of St. Andrew were found in Constantinople, and some of these were sent to Scotland.

SIMON PETER

He was born in Capernaum.

He probably had been a follower of John the Baptist. His name was actually Simon, but Jesus added the term 'rock' which became 'Peter' in English. He was married, and his house at Capernaum has been discovered and excavated.

He was impulsive and assertive...he even reproved Jesus on one occasion (Matt:16,23).

He prompted the decision to replace Judas; and more can be said about him from the Gospel reports and the Book of Acts than any other of the Disciples, as he had a major role in the early church.

His notes of the three years of Jesus were used by St. Mark in writing a lost, esoteric Gospel, as well as the canonical Gospel of Mark.

Church tradition maintains that:

Accompanied by his wife, he preached in Antioch, and in Babylon and possibly in Rome.

His wife was a martyr, and he suffered nine months of torturous conditions in the hideous Mamertine dungeon at Rome. He converted some of his gaolers there.

Death: He was crucified by Nero, in Rome, in an upside down position, perhaps in AD 67.

Tomb: Very early church traditions declare that St. Peter was buried on Vatican hill, and the Roman church claims to have discovered his tomb there, deep underground.

JUDAS Iscariot born in Galilee
Death: suicided in AD 33
Tomb: none

LAZARUS-JOHN (present spiritually)
We have earlier explored a few details about his life.
He was the brother of Mary and Martha who lived at Bethany.
A socially prominent, well-known person in Jerusalem.
Author of *The Gospel of John* and *The Apocalypse.*
Rudolf Steiner reports that all the Disciples were inspired by the spirit of John the Baptist after he was killed; but Lazaros was more deeply inspired by the Baptist.
Church tradition maintains that:
He lived in Ephesus, but left at the time of Emperor Trajan. He went to the island of Patmos, a penal colony off Turkey, but after the revoking of the Domitian laws, he returned to Ephesus.

Death: a natural death in old age in Ephesus
Tomb: Unknown; but at Ephesus in the sixth century a church was built over the grave of a certain "John the Theologian". Just which "John" this was, is difficult to say: John the Apostle, John the Elder, or Lazaros-John.
Site: Cave of the Apocalypse, this cave is on Patmos, between the villages of Chora and Skala, and is believed to be the place where Lazaros-John wrote the Apocalypse.

St. JOHN the Apostle
He was born in Galilee   (and was present physically at the Last Supper)
The son of Zebedee and Salome bar-Zebedee; he was the brother of James the Great.
Formerly he was a disciple of John the Baptist.
He owned a house in Jerusalem, and was a partner in the fishing business with James, Andrew, and Peter.
He is mentioned in the Gospels of Mark and Luke as asking Jesus whether he should, or should not, forbid people to cast out demons in the name of Jesus.
He is mentioned by St. Paul (in Galatians 2:9) as one of the main pillars of the church. Most biographical information about him is not accurate, because this John is confused with Lazaros-John in church records and traditions.
Death: unknown
Tomb: unknown

THOMAS: Born in Galilee
Known for his doubting nature as recorded in John 14;5, and especially in regard to the appearing of Jesus after the Resurrection (John: 20;24-29).
Rudolf Steiner explains that Thomas was less clairvoyantly perceptive, hence was unconvinced at first of the reports about Jesus.
He is identified as the compiler of a valuable collection of sayings of Jesus, *The Gospel of Thomas.*
Church tradition maintains that:
He went to the Middle East and went to India, possibly by AD 49.

Death: in India

Tomb: is at Mylapore a suburb of Madras, and some say there are relics of him at Chennai. Some of the Mylapore relics were apparently sent to Edessa in AD 323, where a memorial site was constructed for them, but in the 13th century these were transferred for safekeeping to Ortona, Italy.

(An intriguing ancient oral tradition exists in Paraguay about him: see Appendix 2.)

JAMES the Great son of Zebedee and Salome

He was the elder brother of St. John. He was a fisherman, and a partner with Andrew, Peter and John.

He was the first Disciple to be martyred, as the New Testament records.[57]

Church tradition maintains that:

He may have been in Spain during his life.

Death: murdered in AD 44, by the sword, by Herod Agrippa 1st, at Jerusalem; shortly before Herod also died (Acts 12.1,2).

Tomb: possibly some body remains are at Santiago de Compostela in Spain.

PHILIP

He was born in Bethsaida.

Like Simon, he has a Greek name, this probably is the result of the policy of the Roman authority (Philippus the Tetarch), to Hellenize Judea.

He was the first Disciple to whom Jesus said, "Follow me".

He was a friend of Nathanael (whom Rudolf Steiner described as an initiate).

All references to him are in the Gospel of John.

In John 6:5, Jesus asks him where is the bread to come from to feed the multitude; but Philip can only give a mundane answer.

In John 14:8, after Jesus states that he "is going to the Father", Philip replies that if Jesus can "show them the Father", then that will suffice for their faith in his words.

Church traditions maintains that:

He was active in Galatia and Scythia, and elsewhere.

Death: he died at Hierapolis, in Phyrgia.

Tomb: his tomb is at Hierapolis, where two of his aged virgin daughters are also buried.

Relics of Philip are in the Church of the Apostles in Rome.

MATTHEW (-Levi)

A brother of James the Less.

He was a customs officer in Capernaum, hence fluent in both Aramaic and Greek; he had become quite wealthy from his profession, which was despised by fellow Jews.

He was not a follower of the Baptist beforehand.

Author of *The Gospel of St. Matthew*, his authorship being attested already in his lifetime.

Church traditions maintains that:

He preached in Judea and in "Ethiopia", meaning northern Greece, Persia, etc.

St Clement of Alexandria reports that he was a vegetarian, and he was not martyred.

Death: unknown

Tomb: in Salerno Cathedral, Italy.

---

[57] Scholars agree that this James was not the writer of the *Epistle of James*, its author is unknown, but quite possibly was James the brother of the Lord.

JUDE-Thaddaeus
He is the person who asks Jesus, in John 14:22, "How is it that you shall manifest yourself to us, and not the world?"
Author of *The Epistle of Jude.*
Church tradition maintains that:
He preached in Iran; in Armenia he is known as the co-founder of their church.
Death: possibly in AD 65 in Beirut, but the Assyrian Church in Iran states it was in Iran.
Tomb: Quite possibly his original tomb was built at Kara Kelisa in Iran, near the Caspian Sea. The western Church has a strong tradition that his remains were transferred to Rome, and are now in a crypt in St. Peter's basilica.

SIMON Zelotes born in Cana
He was presumably, at first a Zealot, which was a vehemently anti-establishment religious group.
Nothing is really known about him.
Church tradition:
There are many quasi-historical traditions about this Disciple, often contradicting the other traditions, placing him preaching in many different lands.
Death: unknown
Tomb: unknown

6 Bartholomew, James the Less and Andrew

7 Judas, Peter and Lazaros-John

8 Jesus in front of a plate wihout a Paschal lamb

9 Thomas, James the Great and Philip

10 Matthew, Jude and Simon Zelotes

Chapter Four: The initiatory Last Supper & the zodiacal link of each Disciple

1: The known meaning: that the Divine has to allow Evil its role
On this level, the painting of the Last Supper event seeks to indicate the dynamics involved in the sacrificial death of Jesus Christ, and with this understanding in the background, to point to the fact of the battle between Good and Evil. In doing this, it also points to how the effort to attain to the Spiritual-self, and even eventually to approach the Grail mystery, invokes a great battle in that soul who is on the initiatory path. Rudolf Steiner commented about the painting, in view of the central dynamic between Judas and Jesus that,

> If a dweller from another planet were to see the picture of the Last Supper, it would understand the meaning the Earth evolution; namely that certain Powers place themselves in opposition to the divine Powers....[58]

Obviously, here he is referring to not only Judas Iscariot, who represents, or indeed is possessed by, evil opposing Powers, but also to the fact that Jesus is fully cognizant of the intention of Judas to betray him, and allows this to take place. So this means the potent and challenging theme of evil as a force which is deliberately an integral part of Creation. These facts reflect back to the situation that evil is part of the comprehensive, vast Idea that lies behind Creation. Without imperfection, or evil, human nature would have been exempt from a Lower-self, and consequently humanity would never experience the urge to struggle towards a Higher-self; and it is in this struggle that a sense of a Higher-self can be born. This dynamic results in the situation that divine Powers, of necessity, had to allow evil to afflict humanity. Divine Powers may well place some limits on what evil beings can do amongst humanity, but they do not seek to fully block evil. This reality is reflected in the words of Christ, when he was about to be arrested by some soldiers, so that the Sanhedrin, after a biased trial, could demand his death from the Roman governor,

> Mt 26:53 Do you think I cannot call on my Father, and he will at once put at my disposal more than twelve legions of angels? But how then would the Scriptures be fulfilled that say it must happen in this way?

These words are anticipated one could say, by a startling passage in the Book of Job, where Satan or Ahriman is accepted as part of the over-all arrangement that 'God' has arranged,

> Job 1:6 One day the Angels came to present themselves before the LORD, and Satan also came with them.
> [Job 1:7] The LORD said to Satan, "Where have you come from?" Satan answered the LORD, "From roaming through the earth and going back and forth in it."
> [Job 1:8] Then the LORD said to Satan, "Have you considered my servant Job? There is no one on earth like him; he is blameless and upright, a man who fears God and shuns evil."
> [Job 1:9] "Does Job fear God for nothing?" Satan replied.
> [Job 1:10] "Have you not put a hedge around him and his household and everything he has? You have blessed the work of his hands, so that his flocks and herds are spread throughout the land.
> [Job 1:11] But stretch out your hand and strike everything he has, and he will surely curse you to your face."
> [Job 1:12] The LORD said to Satan, "Very well, then, everything he has is in your hands, but on the man himself do not lay a finger." Then Satan went out from the presence of the LORD.

One notes here that 'God' converses in a collegial, if frosty, way with Satan, and allows him to attack Job, but placed some limits as to how far Satan may go in this. The theme of evil is

---

[58] GA 132, lecture, 7th Nov. 1911.

extensively commented on by Rudolf Steiner in this lecture cycle. We cannot go into the details of this, but we can note that he describes how the opposing Powers, Lucifer and Ahriman, became deeply involved in the evolving of humanity on the Earth, as a result of 'God' – in this context, the most sublime of the Thrones – arranging for imperfection, and thus evil, to be inherently interwoven into the framework of humanity's existence. This became especially active once the fall into a material-physical body occurred, in the Lemurian Age. The reader will find much help in regard to this theme in Rudolf Steiner's 'Esoteric Science - an Outline', and in many lectures. A sentence from the esoterically inspired German writer, Johann Wolfgang von Goethe, in his drama, *Faust*, expresses the potent dynamic behind the existence of evil, when Mephistopheles says,

> I am a part of that Power who constantly wills evil, but constantly creates the Good.[59]

As Rudolf Steiner explains in, *The Inner Realities of Evolution*, the sacrifice that Jesus makes here at the Last Supper, in allowing Judas to carry out his plans, is a continuation of the great sacrifice of the cosmic Christ being, made during the Sun aeon. In this remote time, the sun-god Christ undertook to slow his own evolving so that he (or It) may in the far future be closer to humanity; that future time is our current aeon.

Leonardo's work from the Akashic Record

With regard to Judas and Jesus in the Last Supper painting, Rudolf Steiner told a group of Members of the Theosophical (later, Anthroposophical) Society, that he had observed Leonardo, from the Akashic Record, painting this great picture, and saw the effort he made in regard to these two figures,

> We gaze at the figure of Judas. The head is dark, and we cannot understand, from out of the picture itself, where the shadows over the countenance of Judas are coming from. So, I attempted on one occasion to penetrate further into this matter, using the means of spiritual research {*the Akashic Record*}. In doing this, I discovered that the painting had not only suffered through the passage of time {*through the centuries*}, and been destroyed, but in addition, that it {*the figures of Judas and Jesus*} had never been painted onto the wall in the way that Leonardo had wanted. For the artist had wanted to paint the heads of Judas and Jesus, in a very particular way….

> For Judas, he was able to use the head of the Prior of the Abbey, but for Jesus he could not find any suitable model. For he wanted really something very exceptional for the head of Jesus, the figure which he eventually painted on the wall never had the appearance that he wanted. Judas he painted with a darkness which came from within himself; a shadow falls on him, the source of which cannot be found anywhere in the environment. He wanted also to paint Jesus with a radiance, which came from within. But this did not become possible.[60]

To have a further understanding of the nature of Judas, we need to note the various little, grey-coloured ceramic salt containers placed on the table. The one near to Judas has been knocked over. Fortunately, we can see this detail in the precise copy made by Giampetrino. In Hellenistic times, salt was very highly valued; our word for 'salary' means salt in Latin, for people could be paid in salt. Salt was able to preserve many of the otherwise perishable foods of that time. Hence salt was used as a symbol of what was valued socially: loyalty and friendship. So, when salt was spilt, it signified in the Hellenistic world, the breaking of a covenant. Here Judas has spilt the salt, so on this level, the painting is conveying the message that Judas is the traitor, he has broken the bond of trust, of fellowship. There is therefore a duality being depicted here: Judas, with his grasping hand and inner darkness, in contrast to Jesus, with his inner radiance

---

[59] In German, „Ich bin ein Teil von jener Kraft die stets das Böse will, aber stets das Gute schafft"; lines 1336/7.
[60] Archive manuscript from the Goetheanum library; lecture, 28th Feb. 1913.

and his hands reaching out to offer bread and wine – his body and his blood – to the Disciples. Now we proceed to explore the esoteric hidden meanings of this painting.

The first hidden meaning of the Last Supper
There are many astonishing and awe-inspiring teachings of a cosmic Christianity in this painting. We shall now consider the first of the more universal, pre-Christian, meanings of this painting, which has to do with the secrets of the primary initiation ritual enacted in secret places of the Mysteries, long before Christianity came into the world. This first, or most ancient meaning, (if we disregard the dramatic emotional quality) is such that if any initiate or member of the ancient Mystery communities had seen this painting hanging up on a public space, there could have been outrage. Why? Firstly, we need to know that the Last Supper itself occurred in an initiation chamber-room in Jerusalem: a room in which acolytes were taken out of their body for the three-day initiatory sleep. And as we shall see, what they experienced there, had some close similarities to one of the meanings of the Last Supper.

2: An ancient zodiacal initiation event
Quite apart from its obvious Christian meaning, this painting is alluding to the secret experiences which acolytes underwent in the old initiation processes. There are two lectures in which Rudolf Steiner reveals in detail the secrets of the ancient three-day 'sleep' initiation procedure. Here is the main part of the first lecture on this subject,

> Initiations in the old Mystery temples, which continued on into the centuries just prior to the Christian era, show us when we gaze inside the ancient Egyptian pyramids, that the esoteric student, when he had progressed {*spiritually*} far enough, so that he could experience love for all of humanity, was placed in a three-day sleep condition....I must describe to you one of the great and significant images {*that was experienced*} in the Mysteries... the person who lay in a three and a half days' sleep was surrounded by {*the vision of*} 12 human figures, amongst whom he saw himself, seated around a table. And just what did these figures represent to that person, who was now an initiate? They represented 12 of his previous incarnations; 12 different bodies, through which he has lived out these lives. In esoteric matters, one divides the body into 12 parts, so these 12 were nothing other than a representation of 12 incarnations, through which the human being is gradually cleansed in soul, and led to a higher stage of perfection.

> Through this experience, the initiate felt himself surrounded by those human forms which he himself had once lived through. He said to himself: the form which you earlier carried around, this lives on in one of your members, in another part there lives the second form, in another the third form, in another the fourth, and so on. These forms surrounded him, like guests at a meal. This was a visionary image seen by every soul in the Mysteries....the highest perfection amongst these 12, was actually with the thirteenth. Because he was outside of his earthly self, he saw himself as the thirteenth.

> Now.... this which was experienced by every candidate for initiation, was once more enacted by Christ Jesus {*in the Last Supper*}. This re-enacting was clothed in a veil, just as everything which is made available externally, that is, exoterically {*of the esoteric truths*} was always enveloped in a veil. The Last Supper, which Jesus set in place with his 12 Disciples, was not an ordinary meal. It was intended to be an enactment on the physical plane of that which so often had been experienced, {*in the astral world*}, by those who were initiated.[61]

---

[61] GA 96, lecture, 1st April 1907.

So from the viewpoint of the first meaning of this painting, it depicts what occurred over millennia in deepest secrecy in pre-Christian times. Below is the main part of the second lecture given on this subject,

> All the various people of the Earth, prior to the appearance of Christ, had their Mysteries. In these, that which was to occur in the future (*in regard to the spiritual journey of the human life-wave*) was revealed. The acolyte was prepared through extensive soul-exercises, so that they could undergo the 'being placed in the grave' ritual (*as it was called*). This involved the hierophant bringing the acolyte into a higher state of consciousness, wherein he was in a kind of sleep state. In olden times the consciousness always had to be suppressed, if the Divine in the human being were to be experienced.
>
> The soul was led through the regions of the spiritual worlds, and after three days was awakened by the hierophant. The acolyte then felt himself to be a new person; he received a new name. He was referred to as a 'Son of God'....Before the time of Christ, the acolyte was renewed through receiving a spiritual spark of the Christ; and it was said to him, "In the future, One shall appear who shall enable all of humanity, to become permeated by Christ, (*as the acolyte had then become*)..." The focus of these Mysteries of the Spirit was towards the future appearance of the Christ. When he thus awoke, he called out, "My deity, my deity, how thou hast glorified me!"
>
> This was how this initiation ritual was experienced in Judaism. The person being initiated saw 12 personalities; these represented the 12 stages of the development of their own soul. Thus there appeared before him, as if externalized personalities, his or her own soul forces. The initiate saw at a certain {*future*} point of time, a very specific scene played out: he saw his own personality transfigured up to that stage where all of humanity is filled with Buddhi {*or Life-spirit*}: in other words, where humanity has become Christéd. He then saw the {*central figure in the scene,*} the deity, as himself, and his soul forces arrayed behind the deity.
>
> Directly behind himself he saw John, who heralded, as the last in this series of forms, the acolyte's {*state of*} becoming perfected. He saw himself transfigured, in a condition which he shall reach when he has become {*spiritually*} perfected. {*This vision is showing*} the personified soul forces in their last stage of perfection: the personality of that John, who announced the Christ-stage {*that is, Buddhi*}. Then in this initiatory sleep, the 12 figures formed themselves into a particular kind of grouping, which people in the Mysteries called the "initiatory communal-meal"....this meal brought to expression the communal linking-together of the 12 soul forces in the human being.[62]

On another occasion he explained that "the acolyte saw the twelve parts of one's body transformed into 12 persons".[63] This statement refers to the well-known traditional allocation of the 12 zodiacal energies to 12 zones of the body; starting with Aries and the forehead, Taurus and the neck/shoulders, Gemini and the two arms/hands, down to Virgo and the stomach, Libra and the hips, and so on, down to Pisces and the feet, see illustration 11. These two texts are immensely valuable revelations of sacred processes, kept strictly secret in the ancient Mysteries. They reveal the first, or primordial, meaning of the Last Supper painting. Let's contemplate the painting from this perspective. These teachings point out that the experience is about 12 past lives and the previous bodies; this means the human life is interconnected with

---

[62] GA 97, lecture, 4th Feb. 1907.
[63] GA 97, lecture, 2nd Dec. 1906.

11 The zodiac and the 12 senses, with their 7 & 5 divisions, and the body areas which each sign governs.

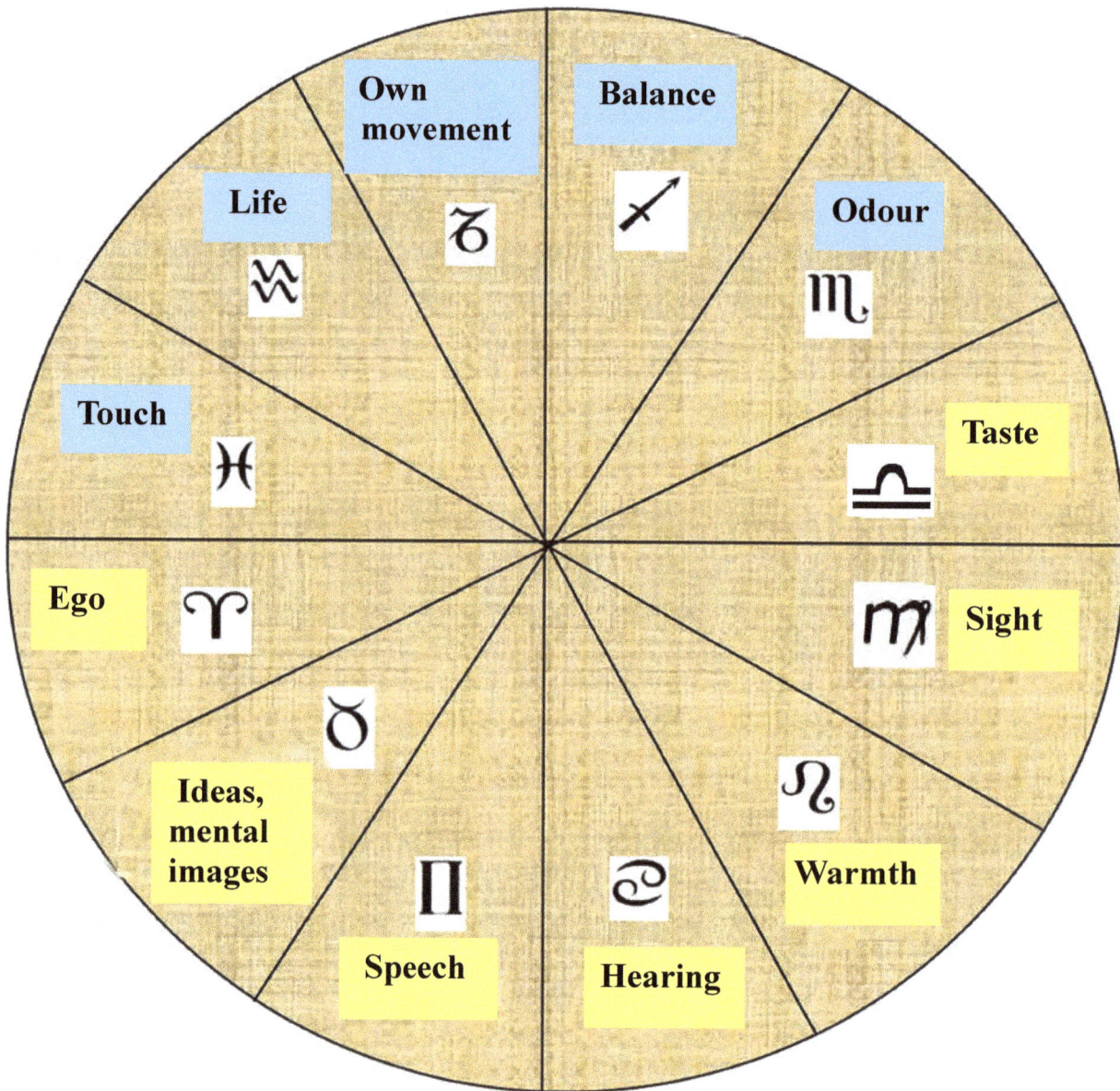

Own movement

Balance

Life

Odour

Touch

Taste

Ego

Sight

Ideas, mental images

Warmth

Speech

Hearing

Blue = night signs, Scorpio to Pisces, still raying down, operative in the subconscious. Also called 'descending' influences as humanity has not yet consciously integrated these influences.

Yellow = day signs, Aries to Libra, operative in our consciousness. Also called 'ascending' influences, as humanity has integrated and ennobled these energies.

Body zones
Aries = forehead, Taurus = neck/shoulders, Gemini = hands/arms, Cancer = chest cage, Leo = heart, Virgo = stomach, Libra = hips, Scorpio = groin, Sagittarius = upper legs, Capricorn = knees, Aquarius = ankles and Pisces = the feet.

the zodiac. That the 12 persons are indeed representing the zodiac is indicated in a lecture in 1905. The brief notes of this lecture record Rudolf Steiner discussing 12 stages of consciousness through which humanity has to pass during the course of evolution. He then comments that, "These 12 are connected to the zodiac".[64]

From this viewpoint, the image depicts the person being initiated in the centre; to his left and right are 12 of his previous life-times. We can conclude that he learns of how his journey through these lives, having different sun-signs, has been building up his self or ego. He has been incorporating the life-experiences that result from being an Aries or a Cancerian or a Sagittarian, etc. He also realizes that in each life he had been interacting with the world, as do all people, through 12 zodiac-derived senses, not just five or six senses. Rudolf Steiner taught that we have 12 senses, many of which are operative at a subconscious or semi-conscious level; see illustration 11.[65] So the acolyte perceives how his earthly life-times, through his sun-sign and his 12 senses, have been a manifestation, down into physical-etheric world, not only of these personalities, but also of the zodiac; the zodiac then becomes a signifier of the Creator.

He experiences how the Word or the Logos has been reverberating through his soul, nurturing his developing ego-sense. The old esoteric saying, "As above, so below" now becomes much more meaningful. Since the highest aspect of the human spirit, which Rudolf Steiner calls the Spirit-human or Atma, is described by him as twelve-fold, this powerful experience is also revealing to the acolyte, the glorious, future, permanent link between the human being and the zodiac or the Logos.

Before we consider the next meaning of the painting, we need to clarify the references to "John", which occur in the second lecture extract. It appears that these refer to that 'John' who wrote the Gospel of that name (and the Book of Revelation). But we know that person is Lazaros-John. So we approach here a deep mystery. We need to note that in the second lecture extract it is said that the Mysteries had a focus on anticipating that future time when the Christ shall descend to the Earth; and that this description is particularly related to what happened in the esoteric Judaic world. So we can conclude that the 'John' mentioned here does refer to Lazaros-John. But this means that the visionary image itself is portraying the future; namely, the future condition of Lazaros, after he has been initiated (or 'resurrected') by Jesus.

That it is itself a vision of the future is clear from what I mentioned in my book, *Rudolf Steiner's Esoteric Christianity in the Grail painting by Anna May.* Rudolf Steiner revealed discreetly that the previous life of Lazaros occurred about 1,000 BC, at the time of King Solomon: he was Hiram the famous master builder. So at the time of the initiation rituals occurring within the Judaic world, Lazaros was as yet, **a future person**; he was still Hiram. So the vision of Lazaros-John representing the acolyte himself or herself at the lofty stage of being a 'Son of God', is really a vision that was anticipating the glorious future destiny of Hiram, as a very important saint within the future Christian reality. For as we noted earlier, Hiram became Lazaros-John, and then Christian Rosencreutz, from whom the Idea or Image behind this painting may derive.
We can now move to the next meaning hidden in this painting.

3 The 12 Disciples share a zodiacal link to Jesus
The ancient classical initiation experience, with its vision of a meal can be applied to the historical life of Jesus. There is an early indication given in a lecture from 1905 from Rudolf Steiner that there is actually a hidden, inner link between Jesus and these men. He told his audience that, "The 12 Disciples represent the 12 consciousness-stages through which Christ {*i.e., Jesus*} has progressed."[66] In this regard Rudolf Steiner mentions that the foot-washing ritual,

---

[64] GA 93a, lecture, 26th Sept. 1905.
[65] These are discussed with a diagram in my *Rudolf Steiner Handbook.*
[66] ibid.

which has various meanings, can be seen as Jesus giving thanks to the Disciples because only through them, that is only through the stages they represent, was it possible for him to attain to his high state.[67] But of course, this reference to "the 12 consciousness-stages..." is an enigmatic statement, which is caused by the very brief notes that were made of this lecture. Rudolf Steiner cannot be referring here to 12 life-times of Jesus, as he was never before incarnated, so Rudolf Steiner's words must refer to a spiritual process. That is, Jesus was inwardly involved, from his place in higher spirit realms, in the life experiences of these 12 men, as they progressed through their various life-times on the Earth. Although Rudolf Steiner does not mention the zodiac at this point, just a few minutes earlier he did.

3b: The 12 Disciples represent the stages on an acolyte's path to the Life-Spirit
Just as the 12 Disciples represented the stages on the path of Jesus, so too can these 12 figures represent the stages of consciousness through which every spiritual seeker in the new Christ Mysteries has to travel, in order to attain to the Life-spirit which is especially the gift to humanity of Christ; just as the Spiritual-self is the gift of the Holy Spirit.

4 A zodiacal link on the etheric level, of the 12 Disciples to Jesus
Those who have read the Gospels are struck by the way that the 12 Disciples gathered around Jesus. He will be walking along and see a Disciple and then say to him, "Follow me", and this man simply stops what he is doing, and follows Jesus. Notes of an archive lecture by Rudolf Steiner from 1905, explain one reason for this. He told his audience that Jesus, prior to his incarnation in Palestine, was able to radiate forth etheric energies into the Disciples, before they were born,

> Jesus was able to outpour 12 etheric bodies as separately existing parts of his own being...his 12 Disciples are his 'members'...**they** are {*the recipients of*} these 12 etheric bodies.[68]

That is, these 12 Disciples are integral parts of the greater, macrocosmic aspect of Jesus, which is his inherent nature through being the vessel of the Logos. The same revelation which Rudolf Steiner is giving here, is recorded in an ancient document recording the words of Jesus which he imparted to his Disciples just a few years after his Resurrection. It is stated in an ancient vellum Coptic text called the *Pistis Sophia*, that the Risen Jesus for eleven years gave spiritual instruction to his Disciples. These esoteric early Christian teachings were somewhat miraculously preserved in this document, although most of it is no longer comprehensible, since its language is of a very specialized, esoteric 'Gnostic' kind.

From the Pistis Sophia
Rudolf Steiner confirms that this is an authentic report of the teachings given by our Saviour to those of his Disciples who, through the gift of the Holy Spirit, had the clairvoyant consciousness necessary to experience Jesus. There is a reference in this text to the Disciples sharing the divine etheric body of Jesus. In this document the following words occur (lightly edited by me for readability), where Jesus, the Risen Lord, is speaking to his Disciples,

> From the beginning I led 12 energies with me, which I received from the 12 Preservers of the 'Treasury of Light', in accordance with the signs emanating[69] from the 'First Mystery' {*the Heights of Devachan?*}. These 12 energies I then placed within the womb of your mothers, as I entered {*down into*} the cosmos {*the astral realm of the solar system,*

---

[67] GA 94, lecture, 6th Nov. 1906.
[68] An unlisted archive lecture, from Haubinda (Germany) August, 1905.
[69] Here I suggest reading κέλευσις as denoting 'sign' or signifier, not 'command'.

preparing for incarnation.} These 12 {*etheric*} energies are now in your bodies. These energies were given to you, from beyond the entire cosmos {*beyond the astral-etheric realms into which earthward-bound souls enter, as required by their karmic debts*}, because it is yourselves who shall save the world. But these energies were also given to you because, through them you shall be able to sustain yourselves against the dangers and threats from the Princes of the {*earthly*} World {*Luciferic and Ahrimanic spirits*}....for all {*other*} people in the world have souls {*derived*} from the power of the Princes of the World; but the power which is in you, that is from me; your souls belong to the {*spiritual*} heights.

This last statement is echoed in an exoteric manner in the Gospel by the words,

> Jn 8:23: But he continued (speaking to the Pharisees), "You are from below; I am from above. You are of this world; I am not of this world...

> Jn 15:19: (speaking to the Disciples) If you belonged to the world, it would love you as its own. As it is, you do not belong to the world, but I have chosen you out of the world. That is why the world hates you.

The words of Rudolf Steiner, and those in this ancient Coptic text, are statements about a 12-fold etheric reality. These also indicate that the painting, in terms of the actual historical Last Supper, in regard to the connection of the 12 Disciples to Jesus, also involves the zodiac.

In Summary
This meaning of the Last Supper painting is that, the 12 disciples are an integral part of the being-ness of Jesus Christ, on the etheric level. Hence when Christ said, "Follow me" to these 12 men, they did, for a part of their own life-forces was speaking to them. Again the zodiac is not mentioned by Rudolf Steiner here, yet we shall see that it is involved.

With the next esoteric meanings we now begin to quote from the unpublished archive document, and apply its words to the painting of the Last Supper.

5 The 12 Disciples as part of the cosmic, spiritual self of Jesus

> **"What in the normal body are the 12 {*zodiacal*} parts, this is what the 12 Disciples are in the 'collective-body' of Jesus Christ."**

In the light of these enigmatic words, the painting now becomes a depiction of Jesus, the uniquely fully divine human being, the archetype of future redeemed human beings, having around him, his eternal, higher ego-sense, represented by the Disciples. The meaning of the expression, 'the collective-body' is not clear, but we can say that it does not simply refer to the etheric forces, as in the previous meaning; it is a more inclusive meaning. It is obviously linked to the zodiac, and so it has to include the mysterious Atma or Spirit-human.

Anthroposophical wisdom teaches that we have three parts to our spirit: the Spiritual-self, the Life-spirit, and the Atma or Spirit-human. The Spirit-human or Atma is the highest part of our spiritual potential; it was brought into being when the cosmic Will that has brought forth our physical body, from God, that is, in this context, from the highest of the Thrones. It exists subconsciously as a will-force within us, and is that part of our higher self or true eternal ego, which is closest to the divine. An initiate of high attainment can access this consciously. The Atma is either what is meant here, or it is certainly a part of this 'collective-body', because the Atma is described by Rudolf Steiner as 12-fold. It is also described as the spiritual force behind the normal ego which is created through our sun-sign and how we experience the cosmos through having our 12 senses. This twelve-fold quality of our ego-sense and eventually of the Atma is brought about by the zodiac forces that have shaped our life experiences, and thus our "I". Rudolf Steiner referred to this astrological or zodiacal reality in various lectures. For example,

> Just as the sun's influence alters as it passes through this or that constellation of the zodiac, so too does the human "I" pass through various phases of its experiences, with the result that in one phase it affects the physical body in a certain way, and in another phase, it affects the physical body in a different way. One feels in Spiritual-science how the sun has different effects on the Earth, according to which constellation it is passing through.[70]

> Just as the sun passes through the 12 constellations, and thus shines upon the Earth from different positions, so too the human "I" shines out from 12 different positions; is illumined from 12 different positions when it gazes back {*upon itself*} from the higher realms.[71]

> Now, there is a certain connection between our "I" here in the Earth and the 12 sensory-realms {*which derived from the zodiac*}, so the "I" lives in a consciousness which is sustained by the 12 sensory 'realms'... we are, through our "I", or {*rather*} **in** our "I", aware of the zodiac...[72]

> This number 12 contains the secret, that we human beings can take up into our being an "I". In that we have developed 12 senses, 12 tranquil regions {*of perceiving*}, these have become the basis of our I-consciousness on the Earth.[73]

These words confirm that our ego-sense, or "I" is being built by our exposure to the zodiac. In one lecture, after going into the details of this, he summarized the interaction of our body and our ego or "I" with the zodiac in this way:

> Physical body: echo of the zodiac
> The "I": perception of this echo of the zodiac [74]

In other lectures he confirms that the Atma lies behind this interaction of our soul, and our physical-body, with the zodiac. For example,

> ...when the human being can master the mineralizing tendency, when he can be master of the skeletal system {*the physical-mineral aspects of the body*}...he shall transform his body into a form which we call the Atma or Spirit-human.[75]

The Atma and the Foundation Stone

The Atma comes about when the will forces that have built up our body, are spiritualized; then the divine Will or intentions behind our very existence manifests in our human will. This power, deriving as it does from the Father-god, is Love; love in the sense of good-will, or a loving intentionality. As such, it is mentioned in the famous Foundation Stone lecture, given when Rudolf Steiner gave the Foundation Stone verse for the first time. There he speaks of the threefold spirit of the human being as the 'foundation stone' of anthroposophy, and describes it as a 12-fold reality; saying that this has its **substance** from 'cosmic-human Love' (the Atma), its

---

[70] GA 62, lecture, 6th Feb. 1913.
[71] GA 119, 29th Mar. 1910.
[72] GA 170, lecture, 13th Aug. 1916.
[73] GA 170, lecture, 12th Aug. 1916.
[74] GA 209, lecture, 18th Dec., 1921.
[75] GA 101, lecture, morning, 21st Oct. 1907.

graphically vivid quality or form, from 'cosmic-human Imagination' (Life-spirit), and its radiant light from 'cosmic-human thoughts' (Spiritual-self).[76]

These words tend to suggest that the entire threefold spirit has a zodiacal quality; and perhaps this is included in the expression, the 'collective-body'. In other words, the 12 Disciples are part of the over-all or 'collective' cosmic soul-spirit nature of Jesus; and this is zodiacal in many respects. The painting is now revealing its profound, cosmic nature.

In the light of this fourth meaning, the question arises: do the 12 Disciples themselves have any real, actual link to the zodiac ? Many rumours exist about this subject; but do we have any specific concrete statements from Rudolf Steiner about this ? Yes, we do: some truly astonishing and specific teachings were given on this subject. Before we consider these, it's worthwhile noting what evidence there may be in ancient Christian texts about the link between the 12 Disciples and the zodiac. There are some references to this in the Book of Revelation, which we shall consider soon, but apart from that, there are only two vague references which I can find.

One is in a document from about 220-250 AD, known as the Clementine Homilies, and states "The Lord had 12 apostles according to the number of the solar months..."[77] The second reference, from about the same time, is found in a text known as the *Excerpta ex Theodotos*, and refers to the ideas of an early Gnostic leader, called Valentinus. It reports him saying, "The Apostles were substituted for the 12 signs of the zodiac..."[78] Both of these brief statements are implying that Christ represents the sun, in some way that is not defined; and although neither person specifically states that the Disciples were directly associated with the zodiac, this is implied. So what then did Rudolf Steiner reveal ?

6 The 12 Disciples each are a vessel of the spiritual energies from a specific zodiac sign

Rudolf Steiner's revelations about this theme are contained in a powerful and remarkable, undated document in the Rudolf Steiner Archives. This document, "*Jesus and his Disciples; the Significance of the Last Supper*", is translated in full at the end of this book, in Appendix 3. Here are his words on this subject, from this document,

> **"The 12 Disciples correspond to the 12 Zodiac Signs {whose spiritual forces} participate together for the ongoing evolving of all of humanity. That which above us is to be found in the stars {*of the zodiac*}, that is expressed there in these 12 specific individualities {*the 12 Disciples*}."**

We need to note here that the positioning of the Disciples in Leonardo's painting is not haphazard, but directly zodiac-related. There are four groups of three persons: this corresponds precisely to how the zodiac has always been arranged traditionally. The four points to the four elements of fire, air, water and earth, and the number three relates to the fact that there are three signs, each of which embodies one of these four elements. So three signs are 'fire' signs, three are 'air' signs and so on. The document goes on to say even more, but first we need to note that there is another implication here to this meaning. For now the painting is depicting Jesus, as the vessel of the sun-god, enveloped in the zodiac, whose energies are present within the 12 Disciples.

So, instead of the anti-astrology or better expressed, the 'anti cosmic star-influences' attitude that prevails in mainstream Christianity, we discover through these words, that each Disciple is spiritually a vessel of one particular zodiac influence ! And we also can realize that of course

---

[76] See my, *The Foundation Stone Meditation: a new Commentary.*

[77] *The Pseudo-Clementines*, in New Testament Apocrypha, Hennecke-Schneemelcher, vol. 2, p. 546.

[78] Greek text in ΕΚ ΤΩΝ ΘΕΟΔΟΤΟΥ ΤΗΣ ΑΝΑΤΙΛΙΚΗΣ;.1.25.2: Οἱ Ἀπόστολοι, φησί, μετετέθησαν τοῖς δεκαδυο ζῳδίοις...

they have to be, because "the Christ", as the great 'zodiacal' Logos, is the Creator of the zodiac. To use traditional language, we are either 'made in the image of God' or we are not. And, as 'servants of God' the Disciples, of necessity, are linked to the zodiac forces. To learn what Rudolf Steiner gave to the world as deep knowledge of the zodiac, as the primary formative force operative in humanity's evolution, and its psychological impact on us through our sun-signs, see my book, *The Lost Zodiac of Rudolf Steiner*.

The 12 Disciples and their Zodiac Signs

Andrew:

There is only one Disciple whose zodiac correspondence was revealed by Rudolf Steiner, and that occurred in a private conversation: Andrew = Cancer. In an unpublished memoir of his life, a German student of Rudolf Steiner, Alfred Meebold from Heidenheim, who believed that he had discovered the correspondence of five of the Disciples to the zodiac, asked Rudolf Steiner about the other Disciples. He answered,

> I can tell you that Andrew is in Cancer. But this knowledge is of no use to you, if you don't discover it yourself. They are listed in the right sequence in Mark's Gospel.[79]

With these valuable words, we discover why Rudolf Steiner refrained from revealing the actual correspondence of the 12 Disciples to the zodiac signs: this theme is about a real, existential, vital reality, because it involves real, existing, initiated Disciples of Christ Jesus, so it has to be approached on a basis of profound awareness of this, with reverence. One has to be very cautious here regarding "listed in the right sequence". For the listing in Mark's Gospel may well be "in the right sequence" – but what sequence ? If one starts with Peter as Aries and goes through the list, the Andrew is indeed correctly allocated to Cancer, but Judas is allocated to Pisces – this conflicts with his nature from the Gospel accounts, and with his other Scorpio correspondence.

Also, since Rudolf Steiner refused to reveal the facts here to Meebold, the list in St. Mark's Gospel cannot be a simple sequence, for if it were, then Meebold would have known immediately to which zodiac signs the other Disciples corresponded to. So the "right sequence" refers to a complex, and entirely unknown situation. So, it is a matter of inner research and awaiting what the spiritual world, specifically the Disciples themselves, from within the higher spiritual world, may or may not bestow upon you as insights.

The suggestion that Andrew is to be connected with Capricorn, because of his hand gestures, is then seen as inaccurate. His hand gestures can now be understood not so much as rejection and confrontation, but as shock (and just possibly a crab-like shape, i.e., Cancerian, quality).

Judas:

We have seen how, in regard to the Last Supper, he is allocated to Scorpio, but does this specifically mean that he is someone who corresponds to Scorpio ?

St. Thomas:

Rudolf Steiner did state in a private esoteric lesson, that Thomas relates to the Age of Gemini or the ancient Persian Age, however this is in the context of a healing miracle related in the Gospel. But it is the case that Thomas in Aramaic means 'twin', and he is called 'Didymus' which means 'twin'; and Gemini means 'twins' in Latin; so it is quite possible that he represents Gemini.

---

[79] Manuscript, Alfred Meebold, *Erinnerungenan einen Geistesriesen*, p. 221, 1933.

St. Matthew:
As we noted earlier, St. Matthew as one of the four Evangelists, has been traditionally correlated to Aquarius. These four refer to the four-fold human being, and the four cardinal zodiac signs of Leo, Scorpio, Aquarius, and Taurus. Possibly this does signify that Matthew is also really connected to Aquarius in the sense that we have been exploring; but this remains unknown.

7 The zodiacal Logos enveloping the solar Logos

We have noted that the 12 Disciples have a link to, or are an embodiment of, a zodiac energy. So, bearing that in mind, the painting now can be regarded as a message about the two great beings which share the name 'Christ"; that is, the highest of the sun gods, or the solar Logos and the great primal Logos, who is part of the Trinity. For, from this viewpoint, **these Disciples now can represent the zodiacal Logos, or, the activity of the zodiacal Logos in humanity**. Whilst Jesus, who was over-shadowed by the great sun-god, and who was through this, the embodiment of the solar Logos, (the Word become flesh), now **represents the solar logos**. So now the painting is a meditation on the zodiacal Logos enveloping the solar Logos: the two-fold cosmic Christ.

It is valuable to note here that these two aspects of the Christ-Mystery are included in the Gospel written by Lazaros-John. For the Prologue is about the zodiacal Logos when it says, "In the beginning was the Logos…" but elsewhere in his Gospel, the solar Logos is depicted. For example, as I revealed in *The Hellenistic Mysteries and Christianity*, in the Gospel of St. John, (9:5) "Christ" is discreetly presented as the sun-god. This occurs in an episode which reports how Christ heals a man born blind. In the normal translations, Christ, through Jesus, says here,

> While I am in the world, I am the light of the world."

But this standard version can hardly be regarded as grammatically correct to the original text. For the translation "while" does not really correspond to the Greek word used here, which is 'hotan' (ὅταν). In the grammatical structure of this sentence, this word almost always means a multitude of times, not just a one-off event.[80] That is, this word means, 'every time that it happens that such and such is occurring.' Therefore, Jesus (or really, the deity Christ, through Jesus) is saying here,

> "Every time that it is the case that I'm in the world, I'm the world's light." [81]

In the exoteric theological world, using the word 'while', this sentence is understood simply as a statement that declares that the ethics of all good people derive in some way from Jesus, who once lived on the Earth. Hence on that one occasion when he was living in the world, Jesus gave ethical 'light' to people. But in his Greek text, St. John is saying that each recurring time it happens that "Christ" is visible in the world, this same being becomes a source of illumination for the planet and its ambient environment. It is of course the sun that recurringly provides this illumination for the planet, each morning. This indication that it is not Jesus but actually the cosmic Christ, a being who derives from the sun, who is meant, takes on more substance when one notes the context of this remarkable declaration.

He is about to heal a man who was born blind – thus, someone has never seen the sunlight. But when this man can see, then he will see in fact the sunlight, because the things we see are only seen because sunlight is reflected off them. Sight is the capacity to perceive reflected sunlight. As Jesus prepares to anoint the eyes of the blind man, he refers directly to the sun, for reasons that are not explained convincingly in any theological studies. He says that he must carry out this healing miracle before night-time comes, that is, before the sun has set:

---

[80] Technically, 'hotan' virtually always means 'each time that something happens' when, as here, the verb is in the present subjunctive condition, and the action of the subordinate clause is contemporaneous with the main clause.
[81] Or, one may say, as the Greek is ambiguous here, "a light to the world", or "the light of the world".

Jn 9:4 "I must do the work of him who sent me, while it is daytime. Night is coming, when no one can work. Each time it is the case that I'm in the world, I'm the world's light." [82]

These strange words may indeed be seen as a distinct allusion to the sun, because when the sun is in the world (in the sky), it is daytime, but when it has sunk below the horizon, it is no longer a source of light for the world. And this solar allusion is even more obvious when we recall that the Greek word here for 'whenever' usually means that it will be a recurring phenomenon, as we noted above. So, this sentence is about the many times light comes and disappears. So the gospel writer wants to suggest that Christ, through Jesus, is saying that he (or rather, It) is the sun ! This possibility is further affirmed by the implication that the healing of the blindness cannot occur during the night-time, for the sun's rays are needed.

And now, we go into the real significance of these truths about the zodiac and the Disciples, for the manuscript goes much further.

---

[82] Some manuscripts have 'I' whilst others have 'we'. The textual authority in the ancient manuscripts is equal for both versions. It is my conclusion, from the context, that "I" is more correct than "we".

56

Chapter Five: The zodiac connection of the Disciples & humanity's future

8 Each of the 12 Disciples is going to become permanently a vessel of one zodiac sign, and so too shall every human being then have that particular Disciple, as their spiritual archetype

This extraordinary revelation about the immense relevance of the zodiac to us is taught in the next section of the archive document,

> **"The 12 Disciples are the 12 {*foundational*} Types of human beings, to whom humanity shall unite, forming groups: and the thirteenth is that person who is above everyone, but who proceeds from out the midst of them. Just as the zodiac constellations exist in a particular sequence in the heavens, likewise shall the human individualities find themselves existing in particular groups, and {*thereafter*} send forth their energies into the cosmos {*as part of a specific zodiac energy*}. Many human individualities shall then consciously gather themselves together into a common grouping; and from {*each of*} these 12 groups eventually a higher reality shall come into being and issue forth its energies {*into the cosmos*}."**

> **.....we find, alongside of the ongoing individualities of the 12 Disciples, also other persons, that is people who are inwardly associated with {*one or other*} of the Disciples; these people form a group or 'host' of souls gathered around that Disciple, just as the 12 Disciples from a host around Christ Jesus.**

> **.... That which each person bears within them as the characteristic qualities of their innermost soul-nature, and also that which each person bears with them as external features {*of their countenance*}: this is what corresponds to his or her {*true*} name – the name which that person bears in the spiritual world.**

This paragraph refers to a future Age when we human beings shall exist in a less physical, more spiritual type of cosmos (a more etherealized Earth in a future Age). The reference to a new name and to a countenance which truly reflects one's inner nature is referring to a future phase of existence. The Book of Revelation hints at all this when it refers to the 'mark of the Beast' or the imprint of the Lamb in a human being, and also when it refers to people who overcome the forces of Lucifer and Ahriman, being given a new name.

> **Thus there exists now, apart from the Disciples, such as Peter, James and John, also Peter-natures (*Peter-people*), James-natures, and John-natures, etc; and these people bear the imprint of that Disciple {*which he or she is associated with*}. Such people also now find themselves coming together {*karmically*}, just as at the time of Christ {in Palestine} the Disciples found themselves coming together. Together, these Peter-, James- and John- people, etc, etc, form a {*spiritual*} power. They already bear the characteristic of a still higher Name {*the Lamb of God*}; therefore when they gather together in the name of this higher Reality, then this higher Reality can be there amongst them.**

> **All the Peter-, James- and John-people, etc, shall in the future join together, and out of their midst, the resurrected Christ, the Paraclete, shall arise. Everything forms itself into an entirety, and the power which through this entirety is active in the world, is itself called, 'Christ Jesus' ".**

Extraordinary revelations; each Disciple is spiritually linked to one of the zodiac signs. They each have a cosmic part to their being, and as human beings develop a deeper, esoteric understanding of the Christ-event, they shall be able to form a unity with that Disciple. Here the concept is presented which we encountered with Origenes earlier, namely that "the Logos is individualized within us". Although this spiritual power of the Logos is within us, it is of course, slumbering; the process of spiritual development is in effect a process that awakens this divine spark within. Summing up the implications of these extracts from the archive document we can see that Christianity is in its very essence, an expression of the age-old, hugely important, influence of the zodiac, spiritually, as mediated by the sun.

The painting is asking the question of the spiritual seeker, who is yearning to enter the path to the new Christ-linked Mysteries: to which one of these Disciples do you now have, or would like to have, an inner spiritual link? **But, no answer is expected to this question** ! At least, not yet, for most people an answer shall only be found in a future lifetime. But to live with this question, and with an enhanced focus on the zodiac is a great privilege, and also a deeply 'Christian' one ! Consequently one should know one's horoscope; and one should know, and work with, the 12 magnificent meditations which Rudolf Steiner wrote about our sun-signs. This situation is a major reason why I wrote my anthroposophical guide to horoscope interpretation,[83] and also included a new translation of the invaluable meditations on the sun-signs, and provided a commentary on them.

In Summary
The 12 Disciples are an integral part of Jesus Himself; they are all part of the 12fold Higher-self or Atma. They were all given a part of Jesus' own ether-body before conception. There is a deep link between these 12 persons, the zodiac Logos, the solar Logos, and Jesus Christ; therefore **they must have a special ongoing task** in humanity's evolution, to do with the awakening in human consciousness of the human spirit. And here this has a specific context: the zodiac energies which have rayed forth from the zodiacal Logos, and which underlie the physical body and hence the Atma. Also, the Christ-light, which rays forth from the solar Logos or the 'sun-god Christ' into our astral bodies or soul.

The future destiny of the 12 Disciples after their lifetime in the first century is not something about which Rudolf Steiner spoke, except for two brief remarks that have been preserved in anthroposophical circles: Firstly, that they all were living as a group in an early century of Christianity, somewhere in the Middle East. Secondly, in about the year 1915, the great initiate Rudolf Steiner stopped suddenly in the midst of a conversation whilst walking up the hill towards the Goetheanum, and his consciousness was moved elsewhere than in his body. He soon became present again, and glancing at this students, by way of brief explanation, commented that, "St. Mark has just died" {and Rudolf Steiner, as a lofty Christian initiate, had been called forth, to be present, as this great saint left his body at the end of his modern era lifetime.}

We can now proceed to the next esoteric meaning of the painting.

9 The moment when the New Jerusalem was born
For those who are familiar with the Book of Revelation, also written by Lazaros-John, the astonishing words which we just have been considering,

> "…..we find, alongside of the ongoing individualities of the 12 Disciples, also other persons, that is whose who are inwardly associated with {one } of the Disciples; these people form a group or 'host' of souls gathered around each Disciple, just as the 12 Disciples from a host around Christ Jesus."

---

[83] *Horoscope Handbook; a Rudolf Steiner Approach.*

will immediately bring to mind, the glowing zodiacal image of the future Earth, and future humanity, as presented towards the end of the Book of Revelation,

> Rev 21:10 And he carried me away in the Spirit to a mountain great and high, and showed me the Holy City, Jerusalem, coming down out of heaven from God.
> [Rev 21:11] It shone with the glory of God, and its brilliance was like that of a very precious jewel, like a jasper clear as crystal.
> [Rev 21:12] It had a great, high wall with twelve gates, and with twelve angels at the gates. On the gates were written the names of the twelve tribes of Israel.
> [Rev 21:13] There were three gates on the east, three on the north, three on the south and three on the west.
> [Rev 21:14] The wall of the city had twelve foundations, and on them were the names of the twelve apostles of the Lamb.

That the city of New Jerusalem is described as having 12 foundations, **with the names of the 12 Disciples** on these, indicates that the seer is describing the same dynamic which Rudolf Steiner is revealing in this special lecture. So, now the painting is telling us that the 12 Disciples shall become the foundations of future humanity, in which the zodiacal Logos has become a tangible part of human consciousness; and this is the New Jerusalem. A brief reference to the 12 Disciples as having become an integral part of a high spiritual existence, is made in a letter written about 110 AD, by a prominent Christian, Bishop Ignatius of Antioch. Ignatius was a prisoner of the Romans, who were soon to execute him. He writes to his congregation,

> "...be eager to do everything in godly harmony: the Bishop presiding in the place of God, and the Elders in the place of the {celestial} Council of the Disciples...."[84]
>
> (Letter to the Magnesians, 6:5)

There is also a brief report of an esoteric lecture by Rudolf Steiner which has some relevance to this same theme;

> The human soul is the fruit of the development of the World-soul {i.e., Logos}...if the World-soul had not developed itself, the human soul could not exist. The human soul must therefore be something, or become something, which is inherently more than the World-soul, something which represents a higher development for this World-soul.[85]

The implication of these profound words here is that the human life-wave, with its zodiacal basis, is of course the outcome of the sacrificial outpouring of the will-forces and the life of the Creator (viewed here as the Logos), the sublime being who created the zodiac. But it also goes on to suggest that as humanity reaches up to its spiritual self, it should actually move gradually on to become a life-wave that brings something more, something new, into creation; thereby expanding the being-ness of the Creator itself. So, the events foreshadowed in the Last Supper, the events on Golgotha hill, now become seen as a time when the Earth would receive a radiance, which in the course of millennia, assists the twelve-sided foundation stone of human consciousness, to become permeated by the cosmic source of its own 12-fold nature. My conclusion here is confirmed by another part of the remarkable archive document about the Disciples and the zodiac,

> **"The Word was there at the beginning: 'All things were made through this same being' (John 1:3). This was the first Christ-sacrifice: he {the zodiacal Logos} gave himself over to the world, in order to call forth the world's existence. Then {following the sequence of thoughts in the Prologue to the Gospel of John}, the Word became Man; it has appeared in a human individual, in a physical body. {As the Gospel of John states, 'The Word became flesh'.}**

---

[84] Ignatius writes "Apostoloen", which is his word for the 12 Disciples; he uses 'mathaetai' for the many apostles.
[85] Esoteric lesson, 28th Nov. 190

> This human being {*Jesus*} who was once existing actively in the world, became an embodiment of all that which the Earth is composed of, in its being and life-forces, {*because*} all this streamed into him, as if gathering together into a point. All single, separate existences {*of the Earth*} were gathered together into this one being {*when at the Baptism in the Jordan, and especially at the Resurrection, the solar Logos, from whom the entire solar system derives, and the zodiacal Logos, from whom the zodiac derives, permeated the soul of Jesus*}."

Once this archetype of the awakened cosmic human spirit, with its zodiacal forces, was created, then he, Jesus, became the perfected 'god-man', whose qualities could flow into countless other people, helping them awaken. So Jesus Christ is the template and example of what a future, spiritualized humanity may become. But: Jesus Christ is also **the source of,** and mediator of, the divine qualities that make possible the Higher-self, including the dodecahedral 'Spirit-human' or Atma. As I mentioned in *Rudolf Steiner's Esoteric Christianity in the Grail painting of Anna May*, a sentence from an ancient Manichaean psalm is helpful when contemplating the nature of Christ Jesus;

"He is the leader on the Path, and He is the treasure which we are seeking."[86]

Earlier, we explored the theme of the duality of good versus evil; of Judas as an opponent to Jesus Christ. But there is another duality hidden here, conveying secrets of the Holy Grail. We can explore this theme by understanding the significance of Judas from a different perspective, as these words of Rudolf Steiner indicate,

> That part which represents the earthly ego, in which egoism rules, which brings death to Christ, is called Judas Iscariot.[87]

It is now necessary that I unveil a secret of the Holy Grail initiation wisdom hidden within the painting; it is important that understanding of this loftiest, and remote esoteric theme, should be known in darkened times.

10 The Holy Grail quest in the zodiac: SCORPIO - LIBRA - VIRGO

Zodiacal truths, associated with the Holy Grail, are interwoven in the composition of the painting. To explore the sacred Grail mystery concealed in the painting, we need to consider again the way that Leonardo was inspired to paint Lazaros-John. We noted earlier that there is a feminine quality to the figure of Lazaros-John, and this fact had led to entirely unfounded, and often deeply improper, mystical speculations about whether this person represented Mary Magdalene. The reason for this feminine quality being incorporated in the Idea of the painting, is actually due to the following.

Lazaros-John: his initiatory state

As Rudolf Steiner describes, when Lazaros arose and walked out of the grave, still wrapped in grave clothing, he had become someone who had attained to the 'Son of Man' stage of initiation, and more than this; his astral body was chaste, purified of earthly sensuality. In the Hellenistic world, those people who achieved the birth of their Spiritual-self, were known as 'Sophia' initiates, because the word 'Sophia' was used as the name of the Spiritual-self; *"the Spirit-self...was called in the secret esoteric schools, the Sophia"*.[88] This state was attained by the Virgin Mary, as Rudolf Steiner taught in regard to this theme,

---

[86] From *Manichaean Psalm Book*, Edit. C. Allberry, Kohlhammer Vlg, Stuttgart, 1938.
[87] GA 94, lecture, 5th Nov. 1906.
[88] GA 97, lecture, 2nd Dec. 1906; GA 100, lecture, 20th Nov. 1907.

Mary, the woman who gave birth to Jesus {of St. Luke's Gospel}, had developed the Spirit-self, over many life-times, and **for this reason she was called "Sophia" by the early Christians.**[89] (Emphasis mine)

Like the Virgin Mary, Lazaros was also now a 'Sophia' person. 'Sophia' means that an initiate, whether man or woman, has acquired the stage of Spirit-self; it does not mean that a goddess is in this person. Rudolf Steiner further explains the reason that the Greeks chose a feminine term 'Sophia' is that,

> the earlier initiates observed how cosmic energies streamed into the pure, newly formed Spirit-self...and hence they gave a feminine name to this fifth part of the human being ....[90]

In other words, with the clairvoyance of the Spiritual-self state, the acolyte felt his or her soul receiving the in-raying energies of the cosmos, and this kind of receiving is a feminine dynamic. Rudolf Steiner further explained that Isis or Sophia was regarded as 'virginal', because the Spirit-self was viewed as virginal, that is, it is not derived from the parents, or one's own astrality...it is fresh and pure, from the divine realms.[91] So in the painting, the figure of 'John' represents Lazaros-John, rather than the Apostle John, even though Lazaros-John is not there in the physical, bodily sense.

That is why the John figure is shown with this feminine quality, to indicate that he is an initiate with the Sophia nature: that is, he has the Spiritual-self born within him. Here we need to note that Leonardo actually listed the Disciples depicted in the picture, Mary Magdalene is certainly not included in his list; the name 'John' is there; so we can conclude that the delicate-looking person is (Lazaros-)John.

But Lazaros was also an initiate of the type known as the 'Son of God'. Although we think of this phrase as a term exclusively used of Jesus himself, it is actually, like 'the Son of Man', an initiatory expression used centuries before the time of Jesus. What it meant was, that not only was the Spiritual-self born now in the initiate, but also the beginning of his Buddhi or Life-spirit stage of spirituality had been attained. With Lazaros, this stage could also be achieved through the assistance of Jesus and the Christ, since Christ, as a solar deity, **is the source of Buddhi or Life-spirit**. The Christ-force in Jesus is that same spiritual force from which Buddhi or the Life-spirit arises. Hence Christ could say of Himself, that 'I am the Bread of Life'. The Life-spirit stage occurs when the astral body is so chaste and pure that the etheric forces no longer have to allow the sensual use of its reproductive capacity; this results in divine life-forces from Devachan becoming active in the etheric body. This grants immense powers to the initiate, for the selfless, loving compassion of the Spirit-self can now become **active** compassion; tremendous artistic and healing capacities arise, and eventually miraculous powers are conferred.

This is why he is known as 'the Disciple whom the Lord loveth': a phrase which means that a spiritual unity has arisen between the Disciple and the Master. This was possible for Lazaros, because his 'Resurrection' was a unique initiation process; the only one which Jesus Christ himself performed, and the last of this age-old, classical initiatory process to be validly performed.

The hidden dualism: sensuality versus the Holy Grail
In the Gospel account, the closeness of Lazaros-John to Jesus during this meal is strongly emphasized. He was leaning on the side of Jesus, and then when he sees Peter beckoning to him, he leans over toward Peter – as shown in the painting – but then he leans back against Jesus, and

---

[89] GA 97 p.58.
[90] GA 55, lecture, 28th Mar. 1907.
[91] See lecture, 5th Nov. 1906 (in GA 94) and in GA 180, p. 29 re Pallas Athene, and GA 97, lects. 3rd Feb. 1907, 2nd Dec.1906, 17th Mar. 1907.

it is then that he asks the question, "Lord, who is it?" We have seen that Lazaros-John, 'the Disciple whom the Lord loveth', has attained to the 'Son of God' stage, that is, someone who has the beginning of the Life-spirit or Buddhi. It is this stage of high spirituality which became known in later centuries as the 'Holy Grail' stage of spirituality. So from this perspective, what is Judas? To answer this, we need to rise above the spiritually uninformed guesswork about this painting, (behind which an anti-Grail influence may be active), which tries to see Mary Magdalene here, and which also views the knife held by St. Peter as indicative of tense, political dynamics amongst the Disciples. For the veiled, sacred meaning is entirely different. Rudolf Steiner, in commenting on the role of Judas in this scene, explains that he represents the sensuality drive, and cosmically viewed, this implies zodiac forces of Scorpio,

> that twelfth part of the human being which represents the Ego, where egotism prevails, that part which brings death to the Christ, it is called "Judas Iscariot". [92]

These comments are referring to the section in the Gospel about the Last Supper, especially these words,

> 13:18,"I am not referring to all of you; I know those I have chosen. But this is to fulfill the scripture: 'He who shares my bread **has lifted up his heel against me.**' "

Now, when Lazaros-John was inspired to write these words, the Greek text was created in such a way that profound initiation secrets could be enclosed within it, to be revealed when it was contemplated with initatory insight. This part of the sentence, 'He who shares my bread has lifted up his heel against me', has three meanings; one obvious, two veiled. The obvious one, clear to theologians, is that Judas has become an opponent of Jesus, where "lifted up his heel" is a Hebrew idiom meaning to be attacking someone. One of the initiatory meanings in this same sentence, referred to often by Rudolf Steiner, and which has been a puzzle for many people, is that it is indicating that the sun-god Christ shall soon become the indwelling spirit of the Earth. This sentence literally contains, for the initiated Christian, this entirely different, cosmic meaning which is hidden inside the Greek words, by a very sophisticated use of the laws of Greek grammar. I have demonstrated that this sentence can indeed be read to mean that; see my *The Hellenistic Mysteries and Christianity* for a detailed explanation of how the ancient Greek text here, and its Hebrew antecedent, does means this.

The third meaning, the second of the two esoteric ones, is about Judas, but now this is teaching that he represents the sex drive. We have just noted above, that Judas Iscariot represents 'the death-bringing egotism, opposed to Christ'. This point was further explained in a question and answer session after a lecture on the Gospel of John in 1907, where Rudolf Steiner comments on the Holy Grail as connected to the purifying of the reproductive force, and refers to Judas as "the lower egotism"; then he comments, "John 13:18 is about Judas, as representing the lower desires, so the sentence is about the Grail".[93] It is this meaning which the great initiate inspiring Leonardo wished to portray in the painting. Judas represents the lower sensuality,

> Whoever is able to contemplate the events of the world {*around about*} them objectively, without prejudice, sees how sexuality can betray the spirit in the human being, can kill it...and one also sees in the Gospel account, how Lazaros-John is placed near to the heart of Jesus; this is to indicate the raising up of the forces of the soul from the lower area to the heart area {*from whence the finest etheric and astral energies rise up to the Grail centre, which is located in the throat area*}.[94]

---

[92] GA 94, lecture, 3rd Nov. 1906.
[93] Lecture of 3rd Feb. 1907, and its Q & A session in GA 97; and the further comment in Archive document #1481.
[94] GA 94, lecture, 3rd Nov. 1906. For more about this, see my book, *Rudolf Steiner's Esoteric Christianity in the Grail painting by Anna May*.

Rudolf Steiner explained to one audience that the term 'heel' here, in its Hebrew origin refers to the sexual part of the body.[95] He was referring to the passage in Genesis 3:15, "And I will put enmity between you and the woman, and between your offspring and hers; he will crush your head, and you will strike his heel."

Iscariot

A help to understanding the veiled mystery here is found in the words which Rudolf Steiner spoke directly after, "*That twelfth part of the human being which represents the Ego, where egotism prevails, that part which brings death to the Christ, it is called 'Judas Iscariot'*". He then went on to say,

> "His name also indicates that he has the money pouch, {*implying*} the avaricious-greediness principle."

However, to my knowledge, his name does **not** refer to greediness. Actually, as regards his name, 'Judas' is a common Hebrew name, whilst 'Iscariot' is a very odd word and its meaning remains a puzzle to scholars. Several different solutions have been proposed, and to me, the one which is most likely, is seen as derived from the Aramaic language and means, 'betrayer'. So what does Rudolf Steiner mean? Twice in the Gospel of John, Judas is named and then described as "He who carries the bag". This phrase was in effect his 'by-name' or epithet, this phrase could easily be meant in a derogatory or suggestive way. So Rudolf Steiner was probably mis-reported, and actually said,

> "His **by**-name also indicates that he has the money pouch, {*implying*} the lower avaricious-greediness principle."[96]

What Rudolf Steiner is hinting at here is the fact that when Lazaros-John refers to Judas and a bag he carries, he uses a very specific Greek word to describe the purse in his sentence, "he carried the bag (or money purse)". This was after all, a purse which Judas would have carried around on his person; and the Last Supper painting depicts him holding onto such a purse. But Lazaros-John uses a very unusual word here: the term 'glossokomon', which does **not** mean money purse. It is a box, not a purse, and in fact, although such an object was sometimes used a kind of money chest, its normal meaning is: **"a container in which the tongues {*mouth-pieces*} of wind instruments are stored"**. Elsewhere in the New Testament, the normal words for money purse are used (e.g., *zone* or *balantion*). So why is this very unusual word used?

The element of the Air and the soul

In contemplating the Greek text here with esoteric insight, one realizes that the high Christian initiate, Lazaros-John, is secretly communicating this truth: that Judas represents the sex desires. For the "mouth-pieces of musical instruments" are used whenever a human being wants to play away happily with an instrument which uses the element of Air, or the wind. But Rudolf Steiner points out that there is a mysterious link between the Air element and the reproductive powers. An outer physical sign of this fact is, that the curled-up embryo in the womb has its reproductive area linked to the throat area. Another sign is the change which occurs in the voice at puberty. As Rudolf Steiner explains, the air is permeated by etheric-astral energies, carried by elemental beings, and these energies permeate our voice, but they also underlie the power of reproduction.[97]

Rudolf Steiner reported that in the far future, reproduction of the human being (when the body is primarily ethereal, not physical) shall be carried out by speech; we shall then intone a new, ethereal, 'light-body' into existence. So a box containing the mouth-piece for playing with the power of the air, is a direct reference to sensual activity. Judas Iscariot – Judas the Betrayer[98] of

---

[95] GA 88, p. 212: The word 'heel in Gen: 3:15 means sexuality.
[96] GA 94, lecture, 3rd Nov. 1906.
[97] GA 181, lecture, 30th Mar. 1918, p.156-161.
[98] Iscariot is probably derived from the Aramaic word 'îs qarya = betrayer.

the Christ-potential in the soul – is that aspect of the human being playing in a self-indulgent way with the powers hidden behind the Air. Hence Rudolf Steiner in two of his lectures, when referring to Judas, also refers to the Air element and reproduction, in conjunction with lower sensuality and as a contrast to attaining to the Spirit-self.[99]

Scorpio - Libra - Virgo:

Now, how does the painting depict these deep secrets of the Grail? What is this knife in St. Peter's hand all about? The answer is that, the high initiate in designing the Idea of this painting **has placed a scene within the scene**. We can be sure that St. Peter is not a Libran personality; he is far too assertive and fiery for that. We don't know exactly what his zodiac sign is, but we can be quite sure that it is not Libra. However, in the scene within the scene, Peter does represent Libra. This is, for the purposes of depicting the Grail mystery and its zodiac aspects, Libra is allocated to Peter; it is this which allows a duality to be depicted between Scorpio, representing potent sensuality, and Virgo, the sign representing modesty, restraint of desire and purity. See illustration 12 where I have clarified how, in this veiled scene, St. Peter has been placed between Scorpio and Virgo; thus temporarily becoming Libra. One can see how there are suggestions of lines around Peter that trace out the sigil for Libra: helped by his outstretched hand above, and lower down his other hand, made longer by the knife he is holding. Notice how Judas is holding greedily onto, not a rigid box, but a soft purse. Notice too, the Virgoan femininity in Lazaros-John, who was not in reality a feminine man, but here represents the feminine Sophia quality, and also the feminine quality of Virgo.

And that is the answer as to why Lazaros-John has his hands clasped together: it is saying, to those with esoteric awareness, that he can conserve his life-forces, so the astral body is now under his control, and thus his life-forces are not subject to those elemental influences which, through Scorpio, and fallen fire elementals, usually dominate the human being. Secondly, the initiate who has attained to the Spiritual-self emanates a tranquil, joyous quality; and this is exactly what is meant when, in the Gospels, it is reported that the Risen Jesus appeared to the Disciples and said them: "Peace unto you".

These words are not meant to simply wish them a restful, stress-free day; for it means, "May you attain to the Spirit-self (or Sophia), for your then empowered spirit has your astral body under control". So, gone is the state of being in servitude to un-freedom, to urges that undermine one's integrity, stemming from Lucifer and Ahriman. And that is a blessed condition which brings deep, tranquil joy, or inner peace. The way that St. Peter is placed between Judas and Lazaros-John alludes to the progress that the advancing spiritual seeker has to make: to leave the lowly Scorpio forces behind and ascend to the pure Virgo state. That is why St. Peter holds the knife and why above, two hands are stretched out: these provide an outline of the lines needed for the symbol of Libra.

This is the spiritual path for those who seek to go beyond the normal interest in spirituality and move towards 'the Grail Castle'. This is advancing by the very demanding task of conquering the Scorpio forces; whereas cultural Christianity is the path of Pisces, which is about learning compassion, empathy and kindliness; hence the symbol of the fishes. Both Scorpio and Pisces belong to the five 'night' zodiac signs, (Pisces, Aquarius, Capricorn, Sagittarius and Scorpio). These are influences that govern the lower section of the body, and are active in the less conscious part of the soul, and in the less consciously experienced senses, see illustration 13. To aspire towards this Grail quest is a more esoteric path, whereas to work with the Pisces forces of being caring towards others is the more accessible, cultural, path. (Although in regard to Pisces, care is needed to avoid being a person so gentle and self-sacrificing that bullying and manipulation are inflicted on oneself.) This Pisces pathway is in many ways embodied in the

---

[99] The sheer sanctity of the Grail Mysteries make them both less accessible and more subject to hostility in decadent times, than other esoteric themes.

teachings of Jesus; but here in a veiled way, the Scorpio path is being pointed out. We note here that both the Scorpio and the Pisces pathways are essential to fully meet the great primary call of Christianity: to develop 'agape', which means a profound powerful love or good-will for all beings. (There is also a deeper aspect to the Pisces path, which is why the disciples are 'fishermen', and why they have experiences with Jesus on a lake, but this is not a theme which we can explore here.)

So the way that St. Peter has specially positioned himself, temporarily, between Judas and Lazaros-John alludes to the progress that the advancing spiritual seeker has to make: to leave the lowly Scorpio forces behind and ascend to the purified, Virgo state. That is why St. Peter holds the knife, and why, higher up, two hands are stretched out: these provide an outline of the lines needed for the symbol of Libra. So this section of the painting depicts the spiritual path for those who seek to go beyond the normal interest in spirituality and move towards "the Grail Castle". This is advancing by the very demanding task of conquering the Scorpio forces; whereas cultural Christianity is the path of Pisces: learning about compassion, empathy and kindliness, hence the symbol of the fishes.

The Christian path to travel along, culturally, is that of the Pisces forces, which teaches being caring towards others. But then care is needed not to become a person so gentle and self-sacrificing that one's own needs are ignored. This Piscean pathway is presented in many ways in the unique advice and parables of Jesus which urge the soul to agape, to selfless love. But here in the scene within the scene, it is the more hidden, esoteric path of triumphing over the lower Scorpio forces which is being indicated. There is a sketch from Rudolf Steiner of a new symbol for the sign of Virgo: a feminine figure which represents the Spiritual-self. For in this figure Rudolf Steiner is presenting this zodiac influence at its best, as the Spiritual-self, see illustration 13. The sketch shows a majestic, tranquil, feminine figure, who is wearing a crown, and has a golden neck-band; these are features which speak of a regal person. And royalty here alludes to empowerment, and when the Spiritual-self is formed, the Higher-self is ruling, it has become empowered over the lower soul qualities.

This figure also has the moon under her feet; this is a specific esoteric symbol for conquering the Lower-self. She is holding a small child who has the globe of the Earth in his hands. This child represents the beginning of the Life-spirit, as well as, historically, the baby Jesus. The same general view of Virgo, as an influence which leads to the Spirit-self, is implied here in the features of Lazaros-John, in Leonardo's Last Supper painting. These higher Virgoan qualities form a strong contrast to the Judas qualities, which embody the negative Scorpio energies. It is interesting to note that there is also another hidden zodiac dualism here; and to see this, we have step outside of the Scorpio - Libra - Virgo feature, and consider the correlation of the four Evangelists to the four Gospels. This is an ancient viewpoint, of unknown origin; St. Matthew has been traditionally correlated to the potential human being or Aquarius, Mark is correlated to the lion or Leo, Luke to the bull or Taurus and John to Scorpio's better side – the eagle. So now Lazaros-John represents the higher aspect of Scorpio; that is, the eagle, which signifies higher consciousness which soars above materialism, becoming radiant. Whilst Judas in contrast, signifies, as we have seen, the astral qualities embodied in the death-bringing, light-hating Scorpion.[100]

---

[100] If a scorpion is placed in a box and exposed to a bright light, it will kill itself,

12 The Grail message: positioning St. Peter to represent Libra

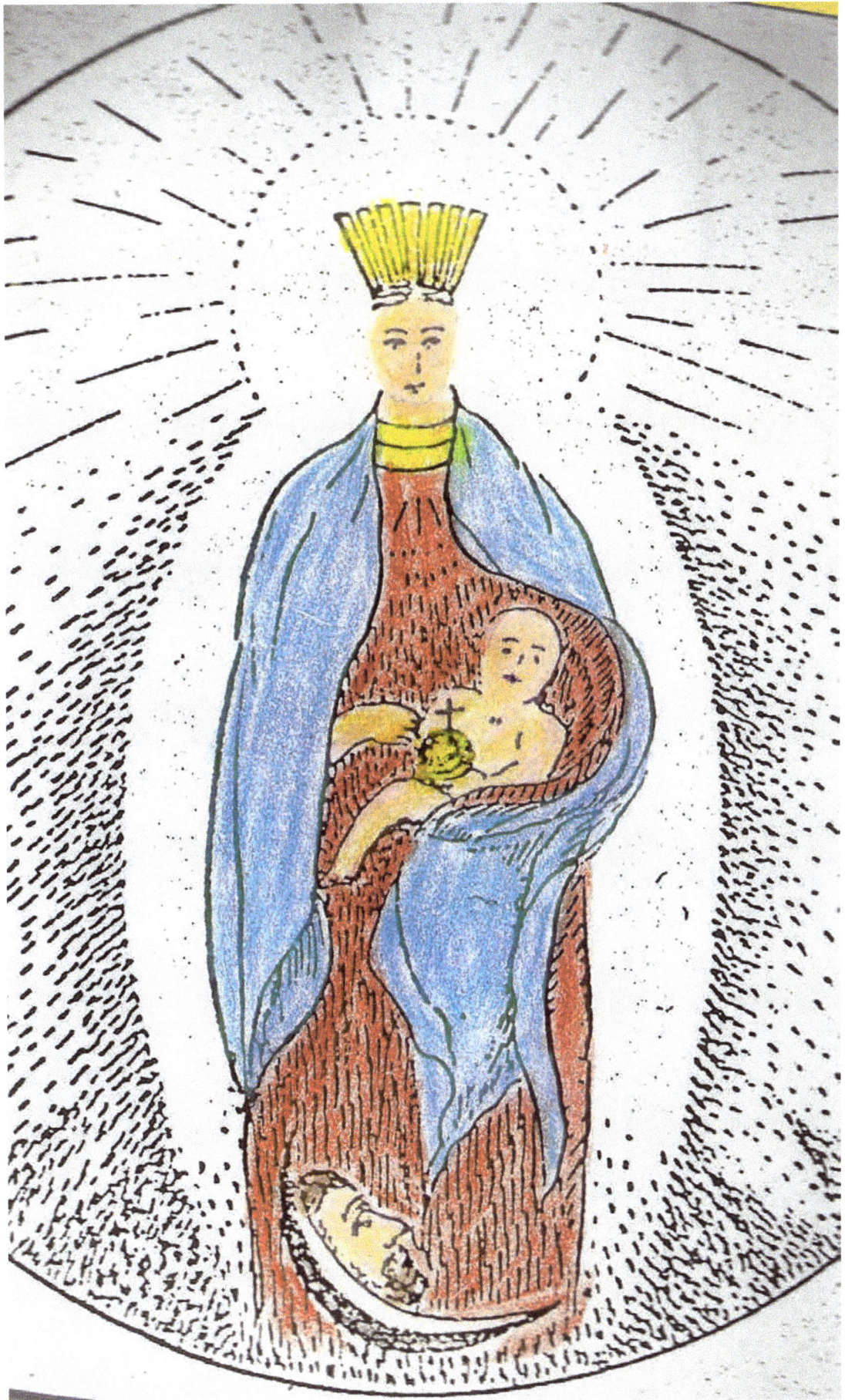

13 Virgo: From Rudolf Steiner's 1912 Calendar (coloured for clarity).

Thoughts on some details in the Leonardo painting

The flowers on the wall:
The mass of colourful flowers may be there simply as ornamentation. But in the Renaissance time, and earlier eras, flowers were considered to be the result of the influence of planets and stars. The great medieval esotericist Heinrich C. Agrippa, wrote about fifteen stars and their interconnection with plants. He taught for example, that Fennel is associated with the Pleiades in Taurus, and sage with Spica in Virgo, and Marjoram with a star in Capricorn. This sense that flowers are associated with the stars, is reflected in everyday language; one flower is called an 'aster', which literally means 'star' in Greek; and there is also the 'stargazer lily', etc.

We are aware that the 12 Disciples each are linked to a zodiac influence, and it seems that the master artist has painted these flowers in the foreground, along with the Disciples – even though they are located in the middle ground. Consequently the three Disciples on the far right have these flowers virtually in their aura (their haloes). But this can only be done by ignoring the great discovery of 'perspective' in the Renaissance, where everything has its right place in space. Moreover, on the right side, several opened doors are set into the walls. It is possible that there is message in these features: the opened portals give access to the starry realm of the zodiac, for the Disciples are inwardly united with the starry heavens. As we have seen, the zodiac signifies the zodiacal Logos.

The hands:
The hands of Jesus are reaching out for the bread and wine, those of Lazaros-John are clasped together in a sign of inner tranquillity, but the hand of Judas has an unpleasant colouring and gesture, which seems to suggest to the legs of an unpleasant crawling insect.

The glassware:
On the table, there are 12 glass cups or beakers, and four glass decanters; all these could be made by craftsmen in the Hellenistic Age. Here the 12 beakers are simply practical items. But the four decanters might allude to the 'four x three' zodiacal symbolism. That is, they may indicate that each group of three Disciples can be viewed as one being: one of the four elements of fire, air, water and earth.

The possible church behind Jesus
High-resolution images of the Milan remnant, made in 2007, has uncovered a building painted behind Jesus, in the distance. One can also see such a building there in the Giampetrino copy; it appears to be medieval or Renaissance church, but neither image is clear. This building might be alluding to a time many centuries after the life of Jesus, when Christianity has become the dominant cultural force in Europe.

The supposed eel and orange slices
Work on the remnant in Milan has uncovered older layers of paint; one of these projects resulted in what may be a plate with cooked eel and orange slices. My conclusion is that this was added during one of the earlier 'restoration' attempts; it was not painted by Leonardo, since it is not in the Giampetrino copy.

68

14   Above: the hands of Judas, Lazaros-John and Jesus
Below: the flowers within the haloes of the saints

Chapter Six: The Disciples and the Bodhisattvas: the Urbino Bodhisattva

Mysterious painting

There exists in Italy a truly astonishingly esoteric, remarkable painting which is a powerful meditation on the theme of the 12 Disciples and the Bodhisattvas of Oriental wisdom. This term, Bodhisattva, is a Sanskrit word, which refers to deeply revered entities, regarded as holy in Hinduism and Buddhism. They are regarded as profoundly sacred, compassionate souls, semi-divine people, who as they evolve further, become a Buddha; so they are lofty souls journeying on to a state of high enlightenment. But their compassion is so great, that they forsake a blissful existence in higher realms, to visit the Earth and to help humanity find the path to enlightenment.

But to fully appreciate the hidden esoteric significance of the painting in Italy, we need to carefully explore it, especially as it has been harmed by recent restoration work. Let's view it, but at first, partially obscured. In illustration 15, I have deliberately removed two figures on either side of the central figure. As such, one would naturally see this as an Oriental painting. One wonders, which Hindu or perhaps Buddhist goddess is this ? Or which spiritual virtue does this figure represent; for the figure here could be a personification, that is, a symbol of spiritual qualities. A clue is given to us, for she is plainly exhibiting what is called a 'mudra' in oriental art: that is, a hand and body gesture which tells the viewer the chief characteristics of that goddess. The mudra which she is depicting here is the "Vitarka Mudra". This mudra signifies 'instructing' or 'educating' in the sense of debate or teaching, a task that the Bodhisattvas have allocated to them. Historically it was depicted with the fingers of only one hand forming a circle, although in recent times it has become two hands. Here, this old painting has a two-hands version, perhaps saying that it is pointing to a powerful source of enlightenment.

And around her head, forming a kind of aura, it appears that we are seeing 12 Bodhisattvas. Some Oriental scriptures teach that there are 12 Bodhisattvas (e.g., the early 8th century Chinese text, *Yuanjue Jing* or the *Sutra of Perfect Enlightenment*). Rudolf Steiner taught that there are just twelve Bodhisattvas; and it is reasonable to conclude that these reflect the influences of the 12 zodiac signs. In any event, the number 12 is associated with the Bodhisattvas in eastern religions. Some oriental scriptures refer to twelve gods who form a host around a Bodhisattva, or to twelve steps to healing as prescribed by a Bodhisattva, or to twelve stages which need to be undertaken in the spiritual journey. How do we understand Bodhisattvas from anthroposophy?

The Bodhisattvas

Let's consider firstly two lecture extracts from Rudolf Steiner about these high persons,

> A Bodhisattva is an advanced human being, someone who has the fully formed Spirit-self, and in whom the first spark of the Buddhi or Life-spirit is developing.[101] A Bodhisattva is a human being whose consciousness is entirely permeated by an inner wisdom {*a conscious knowing*} drawn from his or her past lives.[102]

> Human beings could not actually evolve their spiritual potential further in their lifetimes, if very advanced persons - the Bodhisattva - did not work so as to enable new sources of spirituality to enter into the earthly sphere, gathered from their experiences in higher realms. Between death and rebirth, man ascends to higher Devachan or world of Reason. There a human being, if an initiate, looks into higher realms, realms he cannot

---

[101] GA 89, lecture, 1st Nov. 1904. The beginning of the Buddhi state is also symbolized by the Orobouros serpent, a serpent with its tail in its mouth
[102] GA 60 lecture, 2nd Mar. 1911.

.

15 Celestial wisdom personified, with the Vitarka Mudra.

himself enter, and there he sees the Higher Beings and how they are operative. Whereas a normal human being spends his existence in realms extending between the physical plane up to Devachan {*after death*}, it is normal for the Bodhisattvas to extend to the Buddhi-plane, or what we in Europe call the Realm of Providence.[103]

So, looking now at the partially obscured painting, the question arises, who is this feminine figure, or what does she signify? What link could this Oriental figure have to the 12 Disciples ? To answer this question we need to view the full picture and to then learn more about the link between the Bodhisattvas, the Holy Spirit, the sun-god Christ and the 12 Disciples. So what is this picture? Illustration 16 shows the full picture, as I have refreshed it. As the full painting reveals, it is a Christian work of art ! We see with surprise, that there are two Christian saints on either side of this feminine figure, and we realize that this is not an Indian painting, but a Western work of art; especially as now we can see, although faintly, the figure of the child Jesus on the lap of the central figure. So what is this painting about? It is a fresco, part of a large series of painting, called the *Life of St. John the Baptist*, which was painted in 1416, in the Italian town of Urbino in the Oratory of San Giovanni, by Lorenzo and Jacopo Salimbeni. A very Christian painting, in a very conservative part to Christendom. There is much more to this painting than what we have just described.

How is this possible? How can a Christian religious artwork portray, even if discreetly, the Bodhisattvas and a goddess, or a personification of virtue with the Vitarka mudra? Actually, there are many deeply esoteric paintings from the Renaissance, indicating the inspiration of a high Christian initiate, and the Salimbeni brothers are prominent in this mysterious phenomenon. These two painters, like Raphael and Leonardo, were inspired from spiritual sources to paint sacred, deeply esoteric themes; for example they painted astonishing scenes on the theme of the two Jesus genealogies.[104] No explanation for these paintings is to be found in the writings from the Renaissance; as with the Idea behind Leonardo's painting of the Last Supper, these are the outcome of inspiration from initiates in the Christ Mysteries.

So what does this painting portray ? From the historical viewpoint, we see the Virgin Mary, with the child Jesus on her lap, enveloped in a golden radiance. On one side, holding a scroll announcing the Lamb of God, is John the Baptist, and another saint is to her left. Her Vitarka mudra gestures are in fact both directly pointing to Jesus. She herself however is portrayed as though floating in the air, in a seated position. However, the ethereal, floating quality, and the golden radiance is how she was originally depicted in 1416; this can still be seen in photos taken in the 1980's and earlier. But these two elements are now all but gone, as the painting was "restored" in the 1990's, removing these two features almost completely. Her dress also appears to be decorated with many stars: indicating cosmic or zodiacal wisdom. Around her head is a remarkable aura or halo; for at the top of this is Jesus as triumphant, carrying a flag, whilst the rest of this halo consists of 12 people. These are naturally thought of as the 12 Disciples.

Now, we have already seen that the fully formed Spirit-self is known as the 'Sophia' state in ancient Greece. Rudolf Steiner taught that the Sophia state is also defined as "the personified All-wisdom of our world".[105] Hence, it is very significant to find that Rudolf Steiner taught that **"a Bodhisattva is a vessel of the personified All-wisdom of our world"**.[106] We are starting to close the gap between East and West. He also explained that,

---

[103] GA 116, lecture, 25th Oct. 1909.

[104] The reader may not be aware of the two quite different genealogies for Jesus given in the Gospel of Luke and of Matthew, thus representing two different persons. Rudolf Steiner's explanation for this is not the theme of this book, but the Salembeni brothers have made superb paintings depicting two such boys.
[105] GA 202, lecture, 24th Dec. 1910, p.238 (German edition).
[106] GA 113, lecture, 28th Aug. 1909, p.185 (German edition).

The spirituality present at the Spirit-self stage was regarded, in esoteric Christian knowledge, as a manifestation of the "Holy Spirit".[107]

Therefore, in old languages one would refer to an initiate, especially a Bodhisattva, "as en-filled with the Holy Spirit".[108]

This statement is less astonishing when one learns more about the usage of this term, or very similar terms, in pre-Christian times. For example, Rudolf Steiner explains,

In Asia Minor it was understood that someone who was initiated has some 'spirituality' in their soul. That is, they now possess something higher than the normal astrality, and moreover, that this Spirit-self quality was filled with the *holy* Spirit.[109]

But, very relevant to our theme, on another occasion, and no doubt to the astonishment of his audience, Rudolf Steiner explained that,

The Holy Spirit can also be defined as **the totality of the 12 Bodhisattvas**.[110]

One sees here the cosmopolitan or non-sectarian view which underlies esoteric Christianity, removing the artificial barriers which have been created over two millennia. These revelations mean that the Bodhisattvas form part of the cosmic Christ's reality. In fact Rudolf Steiner explained this in detail, and it is important now that we consider his words, from his lecture cycle, *The Christ-Impulse and the Development of the I-consciousness*, lecture of 25th Oct, 1909,

The Christ is efficacious into the nature of man from the other side of the cosmos – that is, from **these higher realms beyond Devachan**. He is active into those realms to which the Bodhisattvas ascend when they leave the region of the Earth; that is the Buddhi Plane. They ascend there in order themselves to learn, to gain wisdom, in order that they may become Teachers of humanity. There they encounter – coming down to them from beyond that realm, from the other side of it – the cosmic Christ. They then become pupils of Christ. A Being such as He, is surrounded by twelve Bodhisattvas; we cannot indeed speak of more than twelve, for when the twelve Bodhisattvas have accomplished their mission we shall have completed the period of earth-existence.

Christ was once on the Earth; He has descended to Earth, has dwelt on the Earth, has ascended from it. He comes from the other side; He is the Being who is in the midst of the twelve Bodhisattvas, and they receive from Him what they have to carry down to the Earth. Thus, between two incarnations the Bodhisattva-Beings ascend to the Buddhi-Plane; there they meet the Christ-being, as Teacher, and they are fully conscious of Him. The meeting between the Bodhisattvas and the Christ takes place on the Buddhi-Plane. When people progress further and shall have developed the qualities instilled into them by the Bodhisattvas, they will become more and more worthy themselves to penetrate that sphere. In the meantime it is necessary that they should learn that the Christ-Being was incarnated in human form in Jesus of Nazareth, and that in order to reach the true Being of the Individuality of Christ, one must first permeate the human form with understanding.

Thus twelve Bodhisattvas belong to Christ, and they prepare and further develop what He brought, as the greatest impulse in the evolution of human civilisation. We see the twelve, and in their midst, the thirteenth. We have now ascended to the sphere of the Bodhisattvas, and **entered a circle of twelve stars**; in their midst is the Sun, illuminating,

---

[107] GA 96, lecture, 19th Oct. 1906.
[108] GA 114, lecture, 20th Sept. 1909.
[109] GA 114, lecture, 20th Sept. 1909.
[110] GA 113, lecture, 28th Aug. 1909. p.184 (German edition).

73

warming them; from this spiritual Sun they draw that source of life which they afterwards have to carry down to Earth.

How is the image of what takes place above, to be represented on Earth? It is projected into the Earth in such wise that we may render it in the following words: Christ, Who once lived on the Earth, brought to this Earth-evolution an impulse **for which** the Bodhisattvas had to in advance prepare humanity, and they then had to develop further what He gave to the Earth-evolution. Thus the picture on Earth, is something like this: Christ in the middle of the earth-evolution; the Bodhisattvas as His advance-messengers and His followers, who have to bring His work closer to the minds and hearts of men.

A number of Bodhisattvas had thus to prepare mankind, to make men mature to receive the Christ. Although people were mature enough to have Christ among them, it will be a long time before they mature sufficiently to recognise, to feel, and to will, all that Christ is. The same number of Bodhisattvas will be required to develop to maturity in humanity what was poured into the human life-wave through Christ, as were needed to prepare humanity for His coming. For there is so much in Him, that the forces and faculties of people must keep on increasing, for them to be able to understand Him. With the existing faculties of man, Christ can only be understood to a minute extent. Higher faculties will arise in man, and each new faculty will enable him to see Christ in a new light. Only when the last Bodhisattva belonging to Christ shall have completed his work, will humanity realise what Christ really is; man shall then be filled with a will in which the Christ Himself shall live. He shall draw into humanity through his Thinking, Feeling, and Willing: people will then really be the external expression of Christ on the earth.

These teachings which bring the Bodhisattvas or initiates of the Holy Spirit, in whom the Life-spirit is starting to develop, into connection with the sun-god are affirmed in a brief sentence given elsewhere,

> The Bodhisattvas are grouped around the Christ; they have the profound bliss of gazing upon the cosmic Christ – the sun god Christ.[111]

Finally, these words about the task of the 12 Bodhisattvas,

> In the course of humanity's evolution, new ethical qualities arise, but each time such a new capacity is to develop, it must first be manifested on the Earth by a great person...this places the potential in human souls for the new capacity to arise...these great souls are the Bodhisattvas. From whence do these Bodhisattvas gain their special high spiritual qualities? High above in the Buddhi plane, which is above Devachan, in the midst of these high hosts is a Being enthroned, a being who is their teacher and also at the same time the invincible fountain of all light and all wisdom, which streams on to them....the Christ.[112]

We have learnt that the 12 Disciples are each deeply connected to a zodiac energy, and it is also clear that the 12 tribes of Israel are zodiacal. Rudolf Steiner taught that the words spoken to Abraham in Genesis, 26:4, *"For I shall make your descendants to multiply like the stars of heaven"*, (which of course refer to the 12 tribes of Israel), actually mean, that these tribes shall be a reflection of the zodiac forces. Rudolf Steiner explains that "like the stars of heaven" actually means, "in accordance with the twelve constellations of the zodiac".[113] And both the tribes of Israel and the Disciples are part of the cosmic Christ reality.

---

[111] GA 113, lecture, 28th Aug.1909, p. 186 (German edition).
[112] GA 118, lecture, 13th April 1910.

[113] For more about the mission of Abraham and the connection of this to Rudolf Steiner, see my book *The Lost Zodiac of Rudolf Steiner*.

The 12 Bodhisattvas themselves are vessels of zodiac influences, although Rudolf Steiner does not emphasize this, saying simply, "....and **entered a circle of twelve stars.**" (The emphasis here is mine, AA.) But this is an abbreviated expression, which he has used once before **for the zodiac**,

> thus the human being, every night brings, himself into connection with the entire cosmos, the planetary movements and **the star constellations** ... every night after going to sleep the human being experiences himself within all the **12 stars**. Now, these experiences are extraordinarily complex...what you undergo in just one **of the zodiacal constellations** is...[114]

So the 12 Disciples can indeed be understood as linked to the 12 Bodhisattvas, and both to the zodiac. Both are part of the mysteries of the sun-god, but thereby also to the zodiacal Logos; for that is the cosmic Christ reality. These possibilities are relevant to the remarkable Urbino painting.[115]

The Secret of the Urbino Painting

On the obvious level, as required by the Roman church at the time, we see the Virgin Mary with Jesus on her lap and the 12 Disciples around her head, with Jesus portrayed again, with a triumphant gesture. But on the esoteric level, we have a figure, floating in the ether, a **personification** of the Sophia-state or Spirit-self consciousness of a Bodhisattva, in which the Holy Spirit is present. It is this which is the 'mother', or matrix, of the soul of Jesus, as a divine human being. It is this same Holy Spirit or Spirit-self state which Lazaros-John had attained through his initiation, but which was later raised to a higher level, at the Crucifixion. This is referred to the depiction of the Crucifixion in the Gospel of John (19:25-27),

> John 19:25 Near the cross of Jesus stood his mother, his mother's sister, Mary the wife of Cleopas, and Mary Magdalene.
> Jn 19:26 When Jesus saw his mother there, and the disciple whom he loved standing nearby, he said to his mother, "Dear woman, here is your son,"
> Jn 19:27 and to the disciple, "Here is your mother." From that time on, this disciple took her into his home.

Rudolf Steiner reveals that the scene at the foot of the cross, wherein on a normal, human level, Jesus entrusts the care of Mary to Lazaros-John, is also saying that on an esoteric level, Jesus bestowed upon Lazaros-John the divine Sophia quality or Holy Spirit quality which is part of His own being.[116] This interpretation is affirmed by the fact that never in the Gospel does John refer to the mother of Jesus as "Mary", for he is referring to the Sophia or Spirit-self quality. The painting depicts the 12 Bodhisattvas within this divine Holy Spirit reality, encircling her head. Their inspiration is the higher being in whose presence they exist in adoration: Jesus Christ, shown here as an empowered being. And when the babe Jesus becomes an adult, then He who is the source of all the teaching, all the wisdom of the Bodhisattvas, shall undertake his great mission of opening the pathway to the Holy Spirit or the Sophia quality for all those who are seeking.

---

[114] GA 214, lecture, 30th Aug. 1922, London (ps. 179-80, German edition).
[115] It is possible that there are more than 12 Bodhisattvas, and that any others are not in harmony with the sun-god (Christ), as Rudolf Steiner once used an ambiguous phrase, "when the last of the Bodhisattvas which belong to Christ..." GA 116, p. 34.
[116] GA 97, lecture, 2nd Dec. 1906.

16 The full Urbino painting in the Oratory of San Giovanni:
The Life of St. John the Baptist

On one level, it depicts the Virgin Mary with Jesus & two saints and the 12 Disciples; but on another level it depicts the personified wisdom of the Spirit-self, with Jesus and the 12 Bodhisattvas.

From what we have been contemplating here, the question arises as to whether the 12 Disciples shall all become vessels of the 12 Bodhisattvas. I have concluded that this is very likely the truth of the situation, and there appears to be confirmation of this from Rudolf Steiner. For he reveals that the Buddha, Gautama Siddhartha, is very closely linked to the Christ-Mystery. In his lectures on the Gospel of St. Luke. he reveals that the wondrous scene which the shepherds experienced at the first Christmas night above Bethlehem, of Angels rejoicing, were in fact part of the spiritual glory associated with the 'Nirmankaya' or Spirit-self of Gautama. This does in effect affirm that the 12 Disciples are indeed part of the glorious 12 Bodhisattvas who surround the cosmic Christ as a kind of 'heavenly host'.

15 A view of the Chapel with scenes from the Life of St. John the Baptist.

Conclusion

We have become familiar with the primary truths of esoteric Christianity, as presented by Rudolf Steiner, and on this basis we were able to perceive the messages in the Gospel of John about, not one, but two, divine beings who permeated the Earth's aura through the sacrifice of Jesus of Nazareth. So, it became clear that there are two sublime deities involved in the word 'Christ', and that zodiacal influences are intimately interwoven with the spiritual reality of Christianity. The identity of the author of the Gospel of John became confirmed as Lazaros-John, and we came to know something of the initiatory pathway of this great initiate. We have come to understand the deeper significance of the Last Supper in many ways; and the role of Lazaros-John in the Christ-reality.

We saw too that Jesus' own soul, and the souls of his 12 Disciples, are interwoven with spiritual forces from the zodiac. The soul gestures of the Disciples in Leonardo's painting, and some glimpse of their lives, have become clearer, as well as the role of Judas Iscariot in the cosmic scheme of life.

It became clear that the great painting inspired into Leonardo has about 10 different meanings which contemplate the interaction of the cosmic Christ and Jesus and also his Disciples, with the zodiac, and therefore with the great zodiacal Logos. We have learnt that the 12 Disciples are an integral part of the being of Christ, and also of the zodiac. Through all this, the reason for the great painting by Leonardo possessing such power has become clear. The painting by the Salimbeni brothers in Urbino, which presents the inner union of the 12 Disciples with the 12 Bodhisattvas, echoes the cosmopolitan view of the Christ-reality that Rudolf Steiner so courageously presented throughout his life.

From our contemplation of Leonardo's painting, with these ideas in mind, radiant thought-forms can arise in the soul, and from there, permeate the aura of one's locale, uplifting its astral energies and leaving imprints in the ether. These etheric imprints can be sensed by souls as yet unborn, when they descend to life on Earth.

We can be grateful for the help from the great Rosicrucian initiate, Christian Rosencreutz, who has made such paintings possible. As interest in organized religion fades, especially in the western world, the awareness amongst people generally of the existence of the Gospels, and their high moral teachings, could possibly fade away. But if interest in spirituality can deepen and mature, then possibly, esoteric Christian truths, such as is presented in the painting by Leonardo, freed of any church association, and clarified by anthroposophy, may enable awareness of the deeper significance of the Golgotha events to remain known to people on the Earth.

Appendix 1
John's Gospel: Chapter 17; Verse 2
The cosmic Christ referring to Jesus

> And this is aeonic existence: namely that they cognize You (*as*) the only true God, and {that they cognize} Jesus, the Messiah, (*as*) the one whom You sent forth {to humanity}.

Many theologians, and Rudolf Steiner, insert the word 'as', to make this sentence clearer. As you would expect, this sentence has caused huge confusion for theologians; for they work from a view which does not allow the deeper spiritual realities to be part of Christianity. It is of course revolutionary on my part, in the context of this humanistic nature of Christianity, to interpret this verse as the voice of a deity, speaking about Jesus as the Messiah, as the vessel of the cosmic Christ. The esoteric truths of this religion were suppressed or ignored many centuries ago. But only my explanation fits the context; and once awareness of the cosmic dimension to Christianity is realized, it is not some odd interpretation, coming from nowhere.

The fact that chapter 17 begins with: "*After Jesus said this, he looked toward heaven and prayed: "Father, the time has come. Glorify your Son, that your Son may glorify you*", can lead to the conclusion that no-one else but Jesus could be speaking. So many scholars have decided, despite all the strangeness and awkwardness implied by this, that it must be Jesus speaking. Odd theories are created to justify this view. One theory is that Jesus decided to use what would be his future name to instruct people, in advance, as to how to think of him in the future.

But many scholars **do not think** that Jesus is speaking here. These people do use the famous term 'Jesus Christ' when they translate this passage; but they have decided that John, the Gospel writer, inserted this verse himself into the Gospel, as a kind of editor. So, like myself, but for very different reasons, this second group of scholars have concluded that these words were **definitely not spoken by Jesus**. Since such scholars don't know about the cosmic Christ, they have only unconvincing options to choose from to support their view.

To conclude that it is an editorial insertion by the Gospel writer, is as revolutionary as my interpretation, because this is not just some normal editorial work such as the Gospels could contain. This is a potent insertion of words which are very liable to be misunderstood by most readers; the reader naturally thinks they were actually spoken by Jesus. So it is almost alleging deception by Lazaros-John to say that he inserted them, and it is certainly contrary to the entire work-ethic of this Gospel writer, who declared himself to be a true witness (21;24), to think that he is someone who would insert his own commentary, in a confusing, almost deceptive manner.

Rudolf Steiner's commentary supports and confirms my interpretation. In his commentary he firstly indicates the hidden depths of this passage by asking, can anyone who enquires really honestly into this passage, actually find any meaning at all in this 17th chapter? In other words, it is so profound that its meaning is only disclosed to initiation consciousness. As I mentioned earlier, Rudolf Steiner, in his comments on the meaning of this passage, explains how humanity now needs to feel, in freedom, the 'Son-God" (meaning the sun-god, 'Christ') in relation to their innermost "I", and not only the 'Father-God', which people in the old religions have been doing for millennia, (although not so much associated with the "I", as with their group-soul "I").

Consequently, in the course of his commentary, Rudolf Steiner refers several times to "the Christ" as the Being helping humanity here, with regard to a higher sense of "I", because our higher "I" is a cosmic reality. Then, just once in this connection, he refers to 'Jesus', because of course Jesus is the indispensable means by which any dynamic from the cosmic Christ can start to occur amongst human beings.[117] (As we noted earlier, this verse occurs in the context of very profound themes, which I have avoided discussing because that would need a separate book.)

---

[117] GA 345, lecture (to priests), 14th July 1923.

Conclusions from other scholars
Here is a sample of how various renowned scholars view this sentence.

Rev. Heinrich A.W. Meyer, *Commentary on the New Testament*, (1881) thinks that Jesus used his own name here, because "it is a kind of confessional prayer".

Rev. A. Plummer, *The Gospel according to S. John,* (1881) concludes that these words are "not without difficulty", and are an insertion from the Gospel writer and "perhaps abbreviated from {*now unknown*} words of Jesus".

Prof. F. Godet, 𝔎𝔬𝔪𝔪𝔢𝔫𝔱𝔞𝔯 𝔷𝔲 𝔡𝔢𝔪 𝔈𝔳𝔞𝔫𝔤𝔢𝔩𝔦𝔲𝔪 𝔍𝔬𝔥𝔞𝔫𝔫𝔢𝔰, (1903) concludes that here Jesus felt he should "state clearly for once that he is the Messiah, before he dies".

Prof. B. F. Westcott, *The Gospel of St. John*, (1908) observes that these words "present a great difficulty", and remain a puzzle.

Prof. Dr. Prelate Franz Pölzl in his 𝔎𝔲𝔯𝔷𝔤𝔢𝔣𝔞𝔰𝔰𝔱𝔢𝔯 𝔎𝔬𝔪𝔪𝔢𝔫𝔱𝔞𝔯 𝔷𝔲𝔪 𝔈𝔳𝔞𝔫𝔤𝔢𝔩𝔦𝔲𝔪 𝔍𝔬𝔥𝔞𝔫𝔫𝔢𝔰 (1914) brings a complex Catholic perspective, namely that "the one-ness and unity of God does not exclude a plurality of divine 'Persons' ". Consequently Jesus can be thought of as separate from, but also as part of, God. This allows Jesus, in this instance, to set himself aside from God and "require cognisance of God and of himself {*as part of God*}, as objects to be cognized..."

Prof. T. Zahn, *Das Evangelium Johannes*, (1921) concludes that Jesus is here educating his listeners (readers) as to how to understand, and thus address him, once the church has been formed (in the decades to come).

Prof. C.K. Barrett, *The Gospel according to John*, (1955) states that "this verse must be regarded as parenthetical". {That is, that Lazaros-John added these words.} For "John felt the necessity of giving a definition of eternal life to the readers..."

Dr. L. Morris, *The Gospel according to John*, (1995) concludes that it cannot be John who wrote these words, because "why would he do this so late in the Gospel. But {*also it is a puzzle*} why Jesus would not simply say, "me"." But Morris says anyway, "this 3rd person usage from Jesus here does harmonize with the 2nd person usage ('your son', 'him') in the 1st and 2nd verses" {*where again he should have said "me": so therefore all these verses are a puzzle for Morris*}.

Prof. Craig Keener, *The Gospel of John - a Commentary*, (2003) concludes that the 'narrator', John, has added this verse, bringing about "a close association of Jesus and the Father".

The primary source of confusion in the Church over the centuries has been the lack of knowledge of, or the non-perceiving of, the complex and cosmic nature of the Christ-reality; a reality as revealed through anthroposophy. This involves the man Jesus, and various aspects of divine reality, in particular the solar Logos and the zodiacal Logos. As from the early centuries, persons not esoterically aware became the leading church authorities, so this more complex and highly transcendent aspect of Christianity was lost. Consequently the conclusion was made that "Jesus was God". Since the word "God" is in itself a term which is not specific, and is actually inclusive of the activity of many divine beings, this very simplified conclusion accelerated the non-understanding of the highly esoteric, transcendent reality. So there was no chance of this sentence being understood as involving the man Jesus and also a deity. In fact, for many centuries, Church Fathers interpreted the sentence to mean,

> This is eternal life; that they may know You and Jesus Christ, whom You have sent: the only true God.

In other words, God and Jesus are being defined as the same being. This incorrect way of interpreting the Greek is derived from a powerful wish to be faithful to the understanding that "Jesus is God", a concept which is foundational for many Christians, but which is really an exoteric way of grappling with complex esoteric truths. This has been a tendency in Church Fathers over the centuries, using just the usual translation. This attitude of course ignores all the reasons to query why someone (Jesus) would refer to himself or herself as if he were not that same person.

Appendix 2
Ancient Paraguayan and Mexican reports of Apostles

Miraculous events occur, and they occur often in circumstances which proves them to be real, such as by being photographed or even filmed. These are quite distinct from events caused by fraud or by natural phenomena misunderstood through a superstitious mentality. In Mediaeval times, the phenomena of 'bi-location' occurred: this is when an initiate (or saint) appears and speaks at the very same time, to two different groups of people who are living in separate villages. This appears to be the result of the person having the power to project their etheric body, over a distance.

There exist many 'apocryphal' texts, from the early times of Christianity which report strange events connected with the life of Christ, or the years soon thereafter, usually to do with the Disciples. One such text dated to about 250 AD about the infancy of Jesus, full of obviously invented pious stories, also includes the report that as a newborn babe Jesus spoke to his mother. Rudolf Steiner confirms that this report is precisely correct. The language used was a kind of cosmic primal language, understandable only to his mother, (who was a person who had attained to initiation in previous lives).

The southern hemisphere land of Paraguay, a long way indeed from Palestine, was subject to missionary activity in the seventeenth and eighteenth centuries, by the Jesuits. In a report from 1639 about the Jesuit missionary work in that land, one of the Jesuits, Antonio Ruiz de Montoya, wrote, "The Paraguan tribes have a very strange tradition. They claim that a very holy man (Thomas the Apostle) whom they call *Pai Thomas*, lived amongst them and preached them the Holy Truth, wandering around their land and carrying a wooden cross on his back."

Then, many years later, in the 1700's another Jesuit, Martin Dobrizhoffer, in his report of his work in the same area, which was published in 1784, stated that a war-lord said to him, "We don't need for priests, because Holy Father *Thome* {Thomas in English} walked on our homeland himself and he taught us {*their ancestors, centuries before*} about the Truth, praying for us in the name of Jesus Christ."[118] One can of course be suspicious of such claims, especially with Jesuits being known as militant in their approach to their religion. However in favour of the authenticity of these reports is the doubt stated about them, by one these two priests, Antonio Ruiz de Montoya. There are reports of another related phenomenon, which tends to confirm the authenticity of the Paraguayan reports, and which also hints as to what is happening. These other reports are about a much more substantial, and actually verified miracle; it is truly startling.

Jesuit priests working as missionaries in Texas in 1639 reported that native people there were already Christian and that they had been ordered to trek to the white man's camp, where the Jesuits were, to ask for more instruction about Christianity. The astonished Jesuits were informed that a "lovely lady in blue" had many times visited them, and brought the Gospel news to them, quite recently. Extensive research by the Church discovered that a Catholic nun in Portugal, the Blessed Maria of Agreda, was the person involved. She told them of her approximately 500 "visits" to these native tribes, and she could confirm all the details of the geography and customs, etc, of the place in Texas. She experienced herself as moving across the ocean and settling down on the ground, then walking up to the tribes-people. Her Portuguese preaching was heard in the various tongues of the Indian tribes-people.

Such extraordinary miracles were accomplished in all probability by the projecting of her etheric body, across to southern North America; a process caused by spiritual beings. One assumes that her many visits were in accordance with the will of the Christ-impulse, although the Jesuit connection here may give cause for doubt.

---

[118] This is reported in a rare book, *Our Catholic Heritage in Texas 1519-1936,* Vol. 1. Chapt. 7, edit. C. Casteneda.

Appendix 3
Jesus, the Zodiac and his Disciples: the Significance of the Last Supper

   - **Archive notes of a lecture by Rudolf Steiner**

The date and place of this talk are unknown, but it was probably given in Cologne: the place of residence of the two theosophists who recorded and preserved the notes.[119] The notes, preserved in the Rudolf Steiner Archives in Dornach, are very abbreviated, encompassing about four normal book-size pages; whereas the notes of an hour's talk normally fills 25 pages, consequently I have added some additional words in brackets, where necessary for clarity, and also some extensive additional Notes, clearly separated from the text. It begins with a startling revelation, all too briefly noted down by the listener,

(Lecture)
> "Jesus gave his body back to the Earth, when he was placed in the grave {*on Friday 3rd April, 33AD*}, and a short time later, {*on the Sunday 5th April*}, he was resurrected in an incorruptible, transfigured body. When an initiate is laid in a grave {*at his death*} he actually gives back his body {*actively*} to the Earth, so that the particles of his body may permeate the entire Earth, like ferment."

Author's Note:
This last sentence means that the body acts like a fermenting yeast, refining the Earth's physical substance. The particles of a body, lived in by an initiate, become ennobled; that is, the body is made less dense, less subject to ahrimanic coarsening by the presence of the spiritual energies of the initiate.[120]

(Lecture notes continue)
> "Through this {*same process of Jesus making available 'particles' of his resurrected body*}, it was possible {*over the centuries*}, for those who, through their belief in Christ Jesus were united inwardly with Him through the Last Supper, to actually take up into themselves his 'flesh and blood'."

Author's Note:
This sentence introduces a truly remarkable esoteric truth, but one which has to be clearly comprehended, to avoid a really major misunderstanding. It concerns the redemption of the physical body, not only the soul and spirit of human beings. But it is **not** teaching that, through the participation in the Mass or Eucharist, devout Christians over the centuries, literally absorbed the body and blood of Jesus **via the wafer of bread and the wine**. This idea is precisely what some, (but not all), sectors of the Christian faith very firmly insist on. However, Rudolf Steiner explained to the theologians and priests who were setting up the *Movement for Religious Renewal*, later called *The Christian Community*, that this does **not** happen.

So, in the above sentence, there is revealed an astonishing truth about the Last Supper, but revealed in a way that leads to confusion. This confusing presentation is partly due to the very

---

[119] Fraulein Mathilde Scholl and Frau Künstler.

[120] St. Seraphim of Sarov, who lived in Russia in the 19th century, and described by Rudolf Steiner as "a high initiate", left instructions that his body was to be buried (not burned) and that "a wall of spiritual power would arise up to Heaven from it". This same process may lie behind the somewhat unpleasant, but remarkable fact of the incorruptible bodies of some deceased Christian saints.

abbreviated nature of the notes, and partly to the confusion that prevails in all people in the Western and European worlds, who have an interest in a more esoteric view of Christianity; in this case of theosophists and later on anthroposophists.[121] This confusion concerns the nature of the "host" or bread wafer and the wine. The question lives in many devout people as to what really happens in the sacrament; is it possible for the bread and the wine (or fruit-juice, as used in more aware churches) to literally transform into the body and blood of Jesus? The belief that this does really happen was a central idea in Christianity, and the process is known as 'transubstantiation'.

Interest in this theme for anthroposophists intensified when they learned that Rudolf Steiner reported that, when the wafer of bread is prayed over in the sacrament, it acquires a glowing 'aura'. However, in his lectures to the theologians and priests, Rudolf Steiner made it quite clear that the idea of the bread and wine literally transforming into the body and blood of Jesus, known as 'transubstantiation', is not a fact; it does **not** happen.[122] He refers to this concept as arising from a materialistic view of the ritual. He explains that the ritual in a liturgical church service, with its 'holy Communion' where bread and wine are offered, is designed to influence the congregation towards an intense feeling of the underlying idea, namely that the human being can become part of Christ. When such a feeling is experienced, then indeed the soul draws nearer to Christ; but the substance of the bread and wine does not magically change.

So the profoundly esoteric truth revealed here in this lecture, but only briefly mentioned in the notes taken down, is not about the materialistic 'transubstantiation', but about the fact that people who are truly Christian, that is, who accept Jesus Christ as the Saviour, can have the Christ-force permeate their physical body, not only their soul. That is, something of the transfigured, redeemed physical body of Jesus can permeate the physical body of Christians. This extraordinary process is about the gradual redemption of the physical-flesh body of human beings, and it is this process which has its reflection in the theological theme of the 'resurrection of the body'. In anthroposophical wisdom, the physical body is not the same as the flesh body. For underlying the flesh body is a subtle, invisible, spectral form, partly consisting of etheric energy and partly of purely physical forces; Rudolf Steiner terms it 'the phantom', meaning a spectral, tenuous form. Into this form, mineral substance has gradually been absorbed. This is 'matter'; it is our protoplasm and our skeleton, and is distinct from its underlying physical outline.

We have an acceptance of the idea that the **soul** of a devout person can become attuned to the holiness of Jesus Christ; it is said that a holy person has 'the spirit of Christ living in their soul', or a similar expression. Rudolf Steiner explains that at the Resurrection, many 'replicas' of the soul (or astral body) of Jesus came into being, and that what we call 'a saint' is someone in whose soul such a 'replica' of the soul of Jesus, (composed of a ray of divine light), is present.

We cannot go into the details of the 'bodily resurrection' here, except to mention that at the Resurrection of Jesus, countless replicas of his 'physical' body (not the flesh part of it) were also created. Rudolf Steiner taught that human beings can absorb this resurrected or 'redeemed' archetype of the physical body into their own body. And just as people can absorb elements of the sanctity or soul-nature of Jesus, since there are many replicas of this too, such a process requires that the person be a Christian – in a deeper, heart-felt sense, not in a doctrinal sense. So the sentence above,

> "....it was possible {*over the centuries*}, for those who, through their belief in Christ Jesus were united inwardly with Him through the Last Supper, to actually take up into themselves his flesh and blood...."

---

[121] The confusion was deepened by the deeply religious mindset of the note-taker (Fräulein M. Scholl), whose karmic background was that of deep involvement in the church in medieval times.
[122] GA 103, The Gospel of John, lecture, 18th May 1908, and GA 94, 27th Oct. 1906, and in detail GA 346, 6th Sept. 1924.

means that, historically, during their involvement in the sacramental meal, Christians would invoke for themselves an absorbing of the redeemed and healed 'phantom' or archetype of their physical body, sent out into world by Jesus: but **not dwelling in the bread and wine.** By participation in the sacramental meal, the Eucharist or Holy Mass, Christians were being assisted through the ritualistic-liturgical elements, to raise their feelings, their heart, into a nearness to Jesus, thus encouraging and assisting them towards a more chaste, purified, emotional life. This entire topic was explained at length by Rudolf Steiner in his lecture cycle, "*From Jesus to Christ*". There he mentions that the absorbing of the replica of the redeemed 'phantom' is accomplished by involvement in an old religious-meditative practice which formed part of the mystical Christian path many centuries ago; a way of life which was strongly supported by the Eucharist or Mass. These replicas of the redeemed, underlying archetype of the body, exist out there in the planet's aura, waiting to be absorbed by those souls who are attuned to the Christ-being. In this same lecture cycle, But Rudolf Steiner explained also that this redemption of the physical body, through the absorption of a purified replica, is accomplished by involvement in the modern Rosicrucian-anthroposophical path of esoteric development.

(Lecture notes continue)

"Therefore the Last Supper has to remain {*only*} a symbol, until that time when human beings themselves are able to recognize this truth {*that there may come about an inner permeation of one's being by Christ*}. Through the symbolical ritual of the Lord's Supper, people were to be inoculated with a feeling for these truths. Now that the Spirit of Truth guides humanity in all truth, it is possible for the **knowledge** of this truth to be present as well as the **feeling** for it. Whoever **cognizes** this truth, and not only feels it, through this situation, **no longer needs the Lord's Supper**, because such a person daily and hourly celebrates the Lord's Supper through what he or she takes up into themselves physically, and on a soul level, and on a spiritual level. For we do absorb the Christ-existence into us, on a physical, soul and spiritual level. He in us: we in Him."

"The Word was there at the beginning: "All things were made through this same being" (John 1:3). This was the first Christ-sacrifice: that he {*the zodiacal Logos*} gave himself over to the world, in order to call forth the world's existence. Then {*following the sequence of thoughts in the Prologue to the Gospel of John*}, the Word became Man; it has appeared in a human individual, in a physical body. {*As the Gospel of John states, 'The Word became flesh'.*} This human being {Jesus} who was actively present in the world, was an embodiment of all that which the Earth is composed of, in its being and life-forces, {*because*} all this streamed into him, as if gathering together into one point. All single, separate existences {*of the Earth*} were gathered together into this one being. {*This occurred when at the Baptism in the Jordan, and especially at the Resurrection, the solar Logos, from whom the entire solar system derives, and the zodiacal Logos, from whom the zodiac derives, permeated the soul of Jesus*}."

This process was the highest manifestation of that which we recognize as the process in our own soul where we ourselves, in our soul, are a compilation of the external world. For we allow the external world to stream through our "I", and make it into our own possession {*by sense perception and thinking about these*}."

Author's Note:

That is, we interact with our senses in the physical world, with the mineral, plant and animal realms, and our sense-impressions bring about corresponding mental images. This perspective is embedded in the following meditative verse from Rudolf Steiner:

Existing livingly in the cosmos is
the essential nature of the human being;
in the inner core of the human being

is present the mirror-image of the cosmos.

The "I" unites these two,
and thus creates the
true meaning of existence.

(Lecture notes continue)
> "The Word (Logos) in the beginning was divided up throughout the cosmos, {this is what underlies the Gospel words}: "All things were made through this same being". When Christ Jesus incarnated, all things again streamed together into him {*that is, as he profoundly contemplated the world, seeing the essence of all that constitutes creation*}; these things formed again the Word, from which earlier they had been created. After the Word had, long ago, at the creation of the cosmos, divided itself up into all things, these have all become unified again {*in the consciousness of the zodiacal Logos, as it surveyed the life of the Earth, for through descending down to Jesus at Golgotha, the Logos thereby encountered the Earth*}. {*The result of this is that*} the Word could permeate all things with its life. Now the time has come where the life of the Word, the Christ-life, can rise up into manifestation within many human beings, {*who, through spiritual development,*} can bring to consciousness an awareness of the {*indwelling*} Logos."

Author's Note:
These words are made clearer by the following passage from Rudolf Steiner's book, *Christianity as Mystical Fact*, which is actually referring to God, but his profound words here can be applied to the Logos, for it is the direct agent of the Godhead,

> Quote from *Christianity as Mystical Fact*:
>
> These are the teachings which the acolyte received who was to be initiated, in ancient times:
> "*So long as you observe the things in the environs around you, as a logical-intelligent human being, you must remain a person who denies (in your being-ness) God. For God is not affirmed in an explanatory way, to your senses and your intellect. God is in fact, **magically enchanted** in the world. And you require His own power, in order to discover Him. This power, you must awaken within yourself.*"

And then there began for the acolyte the great world-drama in which he became closely intertwined. This drama consisted of nothing less **than the releasing of the enchanted God**. Where is God ? This is the question which the acolyte placed before their own soul.... This multitudinous life {*all around one*} exists, but God does not have **active** existence in them. Rather, he rests within them. {But} He does have existence within human beings. And the human being can come to know this existence of God within him/herself. If the human being is to allow God to become cognized, the human being must creatively release this cognition. The divine, as yet without any active existence, is {*however*} efficacious in the acolyte, as a hidden creator-power. {*The acolyte realized:*} "In this soul {*of mine*} there is a place where the enchanted Divine can again come to life".

End of quote

(Lecture notes continue)
> "The time has now arrived where the Word again calls everything together which has proceeded from him long ages ago, in order to bring them to a state of knowing, to consciousness as to what they {really} are, and what exists {un-awakened} in them. Earlier, the Word gave his own substance to the world, and then {*in the next aeon*} his life, and now {*in our aeon*} he bestows a state of knowing, of cognizing."

Author's Note:
The last sentence is referring to the correspondence of some verses in the Prologue of John's Gospel to the evolutionary journey of humanity through the Aeons,

v. 3: All things through Him were **created**, and without him was created not even one thing, that has been created {and now exists}
      = the Saturn Aeon (when the substance of the physical body was created)

v.4a: In Him was (arose) **life**,
      = the Sun aeon (when the life-force or the etheric body was created)

v.4b: and the life was (became) the **light** of human beings
      = the Moon aeon   (when the radiance of the astral body was created)

v. 5: and the light shines in the darkness, and the darkness did not apprehend it.
      = the Earth Aeon   (when the ego-state was achieved, which has the potential
                          to cognize the Divine)

(Lecture notes continue)

"This third stage is coming now in the form of the Comforter, the Paraclete, which brings about this third stage of the development of the Earth and humanity. Firstly, the Word, with all of its created parts, formed a unified entirety: the Earth was at first, one unified creation. Then the separate parts were imbued with life, but existed still in the Word as a unified entirety. But now the separate parts must become the same as the Word; they have to cognize themselves as a part of the Word, and become a reiteration of the Word. This process is made possible in that the Word now offers up its consciousness, its cognitive knowing, to the world and to humanity. Once the Spirit of Truth has guided humanity in all truth, then human beings, working together can form the Word {*from out of themselves*}."

"The 12 Disciples and in particular the Three {*prominent ones, Peter, James and John*} are those individualities who were the first to consciously begin constructing creatively {*their inner nature*} with the Word. They represent the stages which are required beforehand, which are needed for the building up of the Jesus-Individuality. **The Disciples correspond to the 12 Zodiac Signs which participate together for the ongoing evolving of all of humanity. That which is to be found above us. in the stars {*the zodiac*}, that is expressed there in these 12 specific individualities {*the Disciples*}.** These are the 12 {*foundational*} Types of human beings, to whom humanity shall unite, in groups: and the thirteenth is that person who is above everyone, but who proceeds from out the midst of them. Just as the zodiac constellations exist in a particular sequence in the heavens, likewise shall the human individualities find themselves existing in particular groups, and {*thereafter*} send forth their energies into the cosmos. Many human individualities shall then consciously gather themselves together into a common grouping; and from (*each of*} these 12 groups eventually a higher reality shall come into being and issue forth {*its energies into the cosmos*}."

"From the physical bodies which are left behind, many copies shall be arising; then after a longer period of time, these copies shall be fragmented and dispersed by {*a layer of the Earth's interior known as*} the Numbers-Generating Layer. These fragments or 'splinters' disperse themselves throughout the world, like seeds from a tree, in order to become united, later on, with the bodies of individuals {*who are associated with that particular Zodiacal Disciple*}. In this way each human being bears within themselves a part of the physical body of other individualities, namely those individualities to whom that person is {*inwardly, spiritually*} associated. The 12 Disciples, in regard to {*the spiritual-energy-*

88

body or 'phantom' underlying} their physical bodies, are also dispersed throughout the world – and parts of {*the spiritual-energy-body underlying*} their physical bodies become united with the physical body of people who have an inner union with them. Through this process, certain similarities arise between individuals, {*even though*} each of whom, a long time ago, have laid aside their bodies."

"But also, on the level of the soul, a similar process of splitting-up, and then being widely distributed, occurs. Hence we find, alongside of the ongoing individualities of the 12 Disciples, also other persons, who are inwardly associated with {*one of each*} of the Disciples; these people form a group or 'host' of souls gathered around each Disciple, just as the 12 Disciples form a host around Christ Jesus."

"That which each person bears with them as the characteristic qualities of their innermost soul-nature, and also that which each person bears with them as external features {*of their countenance*}: this is what corresponds to his or her {*true*} name – the name which that person bears in the spiritual world."

"Thus there exists now, apart from the Disciples such as Peter, James and John, also Peter-natures (*people*), James-natures, and John-natures, etc; and these people bear the imprint of that Disciple. Such people also now find themselves coming together, just as at the time of Christ the Disciples found themselves coming together. Together these Peter-, James- and John- people form a {*spiritual*} power; they already bear the characteristic of a still higher Name: therefore when they gather together in the name of this higher reality, then this higher reality can be there amongst them."

"All the Peter-, James- and John- people, etc, shall in the future join together; and out of their midst the resurrected Christ, the Paraclete, shall arise. Everything forms itself into an entirety, and the power which through this entirety is active in the world is itself called, 'Christ Jesus'."

(Footnote)
" From another perspective, one can say that:
Peter also represents the physical body
James also represents the etheric body
John also represents the astral body
Jesus Christ represents the "I" (or ego) "

"Therefore only these three Disciples were present at the Transfiguration, because they represent the stages which lead to the "I". And only once these three were there, could the higher trinity appear: Elijah, Moses, Christ; that is, the Way, the Truth and the Life. Therefore was John placed nearest to Jesus at the Last Supper, because the ego exerts its influence on the astral consciousness first of all, as it is the nearest to the ego. The first stage in the spiritual ascent is thusly the John-stage, therefore John had to be the most deeply initiated. He was the first to experience the deepest initiation. Later there shall be the James-stage and then the Peter-stage. From Peter to the "I", there are three stages of descent; and there shall be three stages also, when the ascent begins, {*from Peter upwards*}."

****

This is the end of the brief notes taken of this remarkable lecture; they are brief, so the ideas are presented in a concentrated manner, and this makes them very difficult to assimilate. But the reader is left with the understanding that the zodiac, as the creation of the zodiacal Logos, and whose 12 influences are rayed down to the Earth by the Sun (the solar Logos), is a primary element of both Creation and our Creators. It is due to the motion of the Sun that the zodiacal energies are active amongst us. By contemplating these notes, we can gradually grasp the link between the Disciples and Jesus with the zodiac; and realize that this link must be really central.

INDEX

GLOSSARY of some central anthroposophical terms

aeon: a long evolutionary time. There are seven of these, and we are now in the fourth such epoch. They are the Saturn, Sun, Moon, Earth (which has two halves, Mars and Mercury) Jupiter, Venus and Vulcan aeons.

Ahriman: an evil entity responsible for the attitude which sees matter as the only thing in creation, denying spiritual reality. It correlates to the Biblical term, Satan.

Angels: spiritual beings who are one aeon ahead of human beings in the evolution.

anthroposophy: a Greek word that literally means 'human-soul wisdom'. In Rudolf Steiner's usage it means the wisdom that can dawn in a person's consciousness, in their spiritual-soul; and which fully manifests when the Spirit-self is developed.

Archangels: spiritual beings who are two aeons ahead of human beings in the evolution.

astral body: the soul, seen as an aura around the body.

astral realm: the Soul-world, above the ethers, but below the Devachanic realms.

astrality: soul energies, but often it refers mainly to the feelings.

BES: the Babylonian Equal-sized Segments zodiac. The etheric reflection of this creates the Zodiac Cultural Ages of 2,160 years.

Buddhi Plane: a divine realm more transcendent than Devachan; where the Bodhisattvas exist

Consciousness-soul: (see spiritual-soul)

Cosmic Christ: the highest of the 'Powers' or sun-gods.

Devachan: the true heavens above the Soul-world; a Theosophical term from the Sanskrit meaning 'realm of the shining gods'; it is the realm of the archetypal Idea of Plato.

the Double: a term usually referring to the Lower Self.

ego or self or I: the sense of self, but the eternal self is linked to this. Hence the ego is a dual or twofold thing.

egoism or egoistic: not quite the same as the well-known term egotism (which means conceit). Egoism is used by Rudolf Steiner to mean either the state of having a normal earth-centred ego, or for this earthly sense of self behaving in a selfish way.

etheric body: is made of the four ethers and duplicates the physical body's appearance, from which organic matter, such as new cells, are condensed.

ethers: subtle energies which sustain all living things on the Earth. Electricity and magnetism are formed as they decompose.

Group-soul: a spirit-being to whom all the animals of a particular species belong.

intellectual-soul: the rational, logical capacity.

Imagination, Inspiration, Intuition: Latin words for the three types of clairvoyance,

but which mean something different in everyday usage in English to the
meanings that Rudolf Steiner gives them.

Imagination: the first stage of clairvoyance; can be called 'psychic-image consciousness'. It
brings perception of astral or etheric images, (usually means 'fantasy'.)

Imaginations: astral thought-forms.

Inspiration: this can be called 'cosmic-spiritual consciousness', perceiving or
'breathing-in' wisdom, from lower Devachan. (In normal English usually
this word means a strongly felt creative urge or idea.)

Intuition: this can be called a 'high initiation consciousness'. It is a perceiving
or inwardly becoming one with another being. This state allows the seer
to perceive at an upper Devachan level. (In normal English this word usually
means a semi-psychic awareness of something.)

intuition: can be used by Rudolf Steiner for the above high seership, but can
sometimes appear in English anthroposophical texts in its usual English
meaning of 'insights' (translating such German words as 'ahnen').

life-force: an alternative term for ether.

life-force organism: the ether body.

Life-spirit: the divinized etheric body, is made of Devachanic energies.

lower-self: the soul qualities that are tainted with Luciferic or Ahrimanic influences.
It can be thought of as threefold, the lower thinking, feeling and will. But
Rudolf Steiner also described it as sevenfold, being the lower qualities of the
seven classical planets in astrology.

Lucifer: a 'fallen' entity who opposes the intentions of the higher gods, creating an
ungrounded, naïve attitude, but also instils a sense of self and enthusiasm for
beauty, art and sensuality.

sentient-soul: the feelings, emotion (aspect) of the soul.

soul: appears as an aura, and contains the sentient-soul, intellectual-soul and spiritual-soul.

Spirit-human: the divine forces underlying the physical body, in our subconscious will.

Spirit-self: the result of the purified and enlightened threefold soul-body or astral body.

spiritual-soul: also translated as 'consciousness soul', and could be called the intuitive
soul. This is the soul capacity which underlies intuitive decision-making or
intuitive flashes of insight. But it is also the most individualized or 'ego-ic'
soul capacity, and can tend towards a hardened self-centredness.

Spiritual-sun: the sun on its soul (or astral) level, behind the physical globe, and also on its
actual spiritual level (also referred to as the Devachanic level): these levels
comprise many energies and divine beings.

thinking: can be used to mean the exercise of our intelligence, but it is also used to mean any of
the three clairvoyant states we can attain.

Illustration acknowledgments

All images are in the public domain

(1. with the assistance of the Royal Academy of the Arts, Piccadilly, London)
(2. courtesy of The National Trust Collections and The Argory, Country Armagh)

Zodiac sigils
These are from: http://www.fontspace.com/category/greek,zodiac,symbols. The use of these graphics does not imply that the owner of these graphics in anyway endorses the worldview expressed in this book.

Also by this author:

Living a Spiritual Year: seasonal festivals in both hemispheres 1992, new edition	2016
The Way to the Sacred	2003
The Foundation Stone Meditation: a new commentary	2005
Dramatic Anthroposophy: Identification and contextualization of primary features of Rudolf Steiner's anthroposophy. (PhD thesis)	2005
Two Gems from Rudolf Steiner	2014
The Hellenistic Mysteries & Christianity	2014
Rudolf Steiner Handbook	2014
Horoscope Handbook – a Rudolf Steiner Approach	2015
The Meaning of the Goetheanum Windows	2016
Rudolf Steiner's Esoteric Christianity in the Grail painting by Anna May	2017
The Lost Zodiac of Rudolf Steiner	2017
The Vidar Flame Column – its meaning from Rudolf Steiner	2017

See also Damien Pryor:

The nature & origin of the Tropical Zodiac	2011
Stonehenge	2011
The Externsteine	2011
Lalibela	2011
The Great Pyramid & the Sphinx	2011

The author's website: **www.rudolfsteinerstudies.com**   has information on all these books, and free downloads and a link to the author's ARTPRINTS page which offers esoteric diagrams and great classical works of art which are relevant to the understanding of anthroposophy.

 There is also a Donate page.

Quality art prints of the 're-freshed' Leonardo painting are available via a link on this website.